Police Management

Second Edition

A. J. P. Butler

Dartmouth

Aldershot•Brookfield•Hong Kong•Singapore•Sydney

Published by
Dartmouth Publishing Company Limited
Gower House
Croft Road
Aldershot
Hants GU11 3HR
England

Dartmouth Publishing Company Limited
Distributed in the United States by
Ashgate Publishing Company
Old Post Road
Brookfield
Vermont 05036
USA

A CIP catalogue record for this book is available from the British Library.

Library of Congress Cataloging-in-Publication Data

Butler, A. J. P., 1944–
    Police management / A.J.P. Butler. -- 2nd ed.
      p. cm.
    Includes bibliographical references and index.
    ISBN 1–85521–215–3 : $29.95
    1. Police administration. 2. Police administration--Great Britain.
3. Management by objectives. 4. Police administration--Evaluation.
5. Police administration--Great Britain--Evaluation.
I. Title.
HV7935.B87 1992
350.74′0941--dc20

                                                                91–37309
                                                                CIP

ISBN 1 85521 215 3

Printed in Great Britain by
Billing and Sons Ltd, Worcester

Unit Beat
Policing
p22-5

Contents

List of Figures and Tables

Figures

Tables

Preface and Acknowledgements

The police service has made significant progress in the past ten years in the areas of operational effectiveness and the control of costs, through improvements to management systems and structures. The service is now more finely tuned and therefore better prepared to meet the continuing challenges of social change and the public's expectation of higher service standards. The process of reviewing the first edition, to consider what changes were required to bring the text into the contemporary context, gave me the opportunity to reflect over the past six years and consider the extent of change in police forces. Although the majority of the book has been rewritten with only four of the original thirteen chapters slightly modified, the new material remains true to the same rational management framework which was the foundation of the first edition.

The rational management concepts of Policing By Objectives were introduced to me by Val Lubans with whom I was fortunate to work before the publication of the first edition. His significant influence on the first edition has continued in this edition with the definitions and principles of Goals, Objectives and Action Plans being drawn from his work. I am also grateful for Val Lubans's permission to reproduce a modified version of the PBO Cycle.

The most significant change to the text has been the extent to which the notion of meeting community expectations through the setting of standards of police services has influenced the structure and theme of the book. At the time I was starting the revision, Mr Michael J. Hirst, Chief Constable of Leicestershire Constabulary was publishing the report of a working party under his chairmanship. The report 'Setting the Standards of Policing: Meeting Community Expectations' was published as the Association of Chief Police Officers' Strategic Policy Statement on the standards and philosophy of policing in the future. The report has initiated the consideration of the 'quality of service' dimensions of policing. The opportunity to work with Mr Hirst provided a stimulating environment in which to consider how the concept of service standards could be pursued and developed in the rational management model. In fact it was implicit in the first edition and the types of policing systems which had been developing in the past eight years. The significant contribution of the Strategic Policy Document was to put it at the top of the agenda.

Although the first edition had had the benefit of being tested in the real world through the work of Mr Maurice Buck, the then Chief Constable of Northamptonshire, my own and others' experience had shown opportunities to modify the text and more sharply focus some of the ideas and concepts. It is impossible to formally recognise the contribution made by all my colleagues and friends but the ideas and comments which have been provided by Mr Malcolm Cairns, formerly Assistant Chief Constable in Leicestershire, and now Deputy Chief Constable in Greater Manchester Police, and Mr Ken Tuckwood, who during the period when the second edition was being prepared was an Assistant Chief Constable in Leicestershire, have made important contributions to this edition. The first edition, and particularly some elements of the structure of the chapters were the result of the contribution made by Karen Cotterill with whom I worked for a number of years. Her contribution can also be seen in the references to her work under her former name. The second edition has also benefited from her comments and support.

Finally, I would like to acknowledge the perhaps unconscious, but nonetheless essential contribution which has been made by all the members of Leicestershire Constabulary to whom this second edition is dedicated.

A.J.P. Butler
Leicester
September 1991

1 Policing for People: Meeting Community Expectations

The last decade has seen dramatic challenges to policing caused by social change and the economic climate. This sense of turmoil has continued into the 1990s. The new challenges are concerned not only with what the police do but how the service is delivered. Public confidence in the police is said to be declining. An issue in the debate about 'what has gone wrong' is the question of the role of leadership as opposed to management. It has been said that too much management is the problem with policing: what is needed is more leadership. This debate is not likely to be very productive because the issue is not one of labels; it is a matter of creating opportunities for staff to achieve their full potential in pursuit of the mission of the police force. In fact to debate the problems at this level illustrates the superficial understanding of the real issues. These are the issues which must be considered to enable police forces to respond to the current criticisms and challenges:

1 A vision of what the police force is attempting to achieve in its response to community expectations.
2 A recognition by the Chief Constable of the problems to be solved to achieve the vision.
3 A commitment by the Chief Constable to implement the process to achieve the vision.
4 A sense of mission shared by all members of the force.
5 A structure which allows people closest to the problem to make the decisions to solve it.
6 Systems and procedures which enhance the opportunities for staff to achieve their full potential.
7 A commitment to excellence.
8 A system of management which allows results to be measured and the lessons of the past used to guide actions in the future.

Vision and excellence are seen as the prerogative of the leader, with matters such as systems and procedures and the measurement of results being the hallmarks of the manager. The reality of achieving the mission makes these distinctions arbitrary and misleading, which distracts attention from the real issue, namely the need to achieve results. Leadership and management are two sides of the same coin. Leadership is concerned with the vision and creating a sense of shared mission and confidence in staff that the mission can be achieved. Management ensures that the planning, organising of resources, implementation and evaluation are carried through to achieve the leader's vision. The manager and leader share one goal, the achievement of results consistent with the mission of the police force: therefore this book will treat the two concepts as one.

Police management strategy should seek two goals: first, to provide a better, more challenging and fulfilling job for all members of the force, and second, to improve the effectiveness and efficiency of the force, thereby improving the quality of the service provided to the community. Improvements in performance rely entirely on the staff. Their commitment is critical. To ask staff to change their working practices or to become more productive, without offering them the opportunity to have some benefits from the changes, is to be rather shortsighted. Successful police management systems are based on devolved decision making because the staff most likely to know the solution to the policing problem will be those who are closest to it. Therefore they should be given the greatest opportunity to make the decisions to solve the problem. This policy will bring advantages to the force by developing a more responsive and flexible organisation. It will also bring advantages to the individuals involved because it will give them more control over their world, bringing more opportunities to achieve a sense of personal satisfaction from their work and give them opportunities to develop management skills to improve their prospects of advancement. Thus the policy will achieve the two goals of improving the working environment of individuals and the performance of the force.

Introducing the Book

The purpose of this book is to explore practical methods of improving the delivery of services to the community. Although there is a current enthusiasm for the concept of quality of service, the critical issue is the extent to which police forces satisfy the expectations of the community. The caring, polite and reassuring style of policing is an essential part of meeting the expectations of the public. In addition the community also expects the police force to be effective in combating armed robberies, fraud and football hooligans, and to make the best use of their resources. Therefore police forces must strive to be seen in the eyes of the community as operationally effective, efficient users of resources and deliver services to a quality that meets their expectations. These are all dimensions of the judgements the public will make in determining their satisfaction with, and confidence in, the police service they receive.

The contents and sequence of the chapters form a working guide to the stages and processes which will enable a police force to make better use of its resources and measure the results it achieves. Practical police problems are examined in case studies to show how management concepts can be applied to police work to achieve improvements in performance. It is essential that each part of the process is understood and related to the actual experience of the reader. The essential management concepts and issues have been summarised as *key points* at the beginning of each chapter.

Before significant improvements in performance can be achieved, additional training will be required for many police officers. This could be provided in formal training sessions or through a process of action learning 'on-the-job'. The key points can provide the basic framework for this training and will be useful to an officer who has the task of designing training courses. The key points also provide a valuable guide for any sub-divisional superintendent who wishes to improve the performance of his sub-division, by defining the concepts and issues which must be understood by his staff. He can take the chapter and the key points and design his own training package for an action learning approach.

Within an operational context, this book is concerned with officers who have management responsibilities. Attention will tend to be directed towards the sub-division as the primary operational unit and the term 'police manager' will usually refer to the sub-divisional superintendent, but police managers may be located at almost any point in the police force, because the term is a generic one used to denote any officer or civilian member of staff who has responsibility for controlling the activities of others towards some defined target or goal.

The principles and concepts will be described in the context of a typical British police force. Allowances will have to be made for local variations which will not affect the principles but may necessitate some modifications in the process of application.

The key points of this chapter are:

1   To understand the need for a rational approach to police management to bring a structured and disciplined framework to problem solving.
2   To understand the two goals of management development in the police: improving the working environment of staff and the performance of the force.
3   To understand the value of developing policing strategies as a response to community expectations.
4   To recognise the limitations of current police management practice.
5   To understand the definition of quality.

Policing for People

Public consultation has risen to prominence since the publication of Lord Scarman's report in 1981.[1] Consultation by itself will not result in improved police services unless the consultation process is formally recognised as part of the corporate planning strategy. Methods by which this can be achieved will be discussed later, but at this point it is important to recognise that the process must be sufficiently sophisticated to ensure that all groups and levels in society have an opportunity to make a contribution. Consultation is not an end in itself but a means to provide an opportunity to improve police service delivery. Consultation should not be seen from the narrow perspective of the formal process of public meetings, but as the generic term for the process of determining community expectations, monitoring service delivery standards and marketing the results of police actions back to the community.

In a review of Unit Beat Policing (UBP) in Chapter 2, it will be argued that it was shortcomings in police management that was the critical deficiency in the introduction of UBP; the policy, implicit in the concept, was determined almost exclusively by central government. The Home Office sponsored the Working Party which produced the report recommending the system. After the publication of the report, the Home Office enthusiastically encouraged chief officers to take advantage of new technology and provided the offer of financial assistance as incentives for the purchase of personal radios

Policy?

and cars. Local communities were not directly involved or consulted in the design or implementation of Unit Beat Policing, but when public concern was expressed it did not, apparently, influence policy. At the time Unit Beat Policing was designed, the police and government were facing the problem of continuing to provide a service with static or decreasing manpower. If the police had applied the rational management principle of problem analysis and planning to the government's recommendation to implement Unit Beat Policing, the model would have been modified to meet the needs of the community within the available resources. Unfortunately the police passively accepted the model and attempted to stretch resources. As a result the first priority of the police, responding to calls for service, inevitably took precedence over the second priority, maintaining contact with the community through area foot patrol constables.

Unfortunately the police service is still vulnerable to the damage which can be done by a Chief Constable imposing a solution without considering the problem. The alternative approach to providing police services is to establish a mission based on meeting community expectations to create basic operational units, to provide resources for these units and then to make sub-divisional commanders responsible for delivering services to agreed standards. This book prescribes the application of this alternative approach because it creates the opportunities for people to receive the police services they need. The former approach can become a straitjacket which is not responsive to the specific needs of diverse communities.

There may be some value in debating the future role of the police from the constitutional or philosophical viewpoint, but in the meantime services continue to be provided. Unfortunately public opinion surveys show that the largest decline in public confidence is found among people who have been in contact with the police. It appears that it is not what the police are doing which is causing a problem, it is how they are doing it. The superficial response would be to jump to the solution of making police officers more polite and caring, but this would be another example of the classic error of imposing a solution before the problem has been analysed to identify causes. Three examples illustrate some of the issues.

Case A: Who Owns the Problem?

A woman driving her car was hit from behind while she was waiting in a queue of traffic. When she spoke to the other driver he was abusive and drove off without giving any information. She took the number and a witness gave her his name and address. She reported the accident to her local police station. After a few weeks she had not heard anything from the police. She called the station where she had reported the accident, to be told that all accidents were handled by a central unit; she was advised to call them. She called this number and was told that there was no record of the accident; she was advised to call the original station. When she called the station she was asked the identity of the officer to whom she had made the original report. Unable to recall the name of the officer she was asked if she could remember the date and time of the report. When she said she could, the woman was told to call another number in the morning to speak to the person who was responsible for the personnel shift records. Following instructions, she called the number and explained the problem. The clerk said she would give her the names of all the officers who were on duty when she made the original report, and then she could ring them to ask if they remembered her reporting the accident. Unfortunately the first time the woman called to speak to an officer she was told he had moved to another station. In desperation she called the accident administration unit. On this occasion a clerk took responsibility for solving the woman's problem and made arrangements for an officer to call to see her to re-record the information in order to investigate the accident.

Case B: What's the Problem? The Accident was Investigated

A man was badly injured in a road accident and four months later, still in hospital, he met, by chance, a police officer who was visiting another patient. The man explained that since the accident he had been in hospital and had had no contact with the police. He did not know if the other driver had been traced or any other details about the incident. The officer promised to ensure he was given this information. On making enquiries the officer discovered that the accident had been reconstructed by trained accident investigators, the other driver had been traced and interviewed, a file had been prepared and summonses issued against him. The only thing not done was to provide this information to the injured man.

Case C: 'Don't Blame Me, it's the System'

Complaints were being received about delays in the arrival of scenes of crime officers (SOCOs). For example, officers who attended the scene of a burglary told the victim to expect a visit from the SOCO and to leave the scene undisturbed. The officers informed the control room of the need for a SOCO. The control room called the SOCO over the radio and told him of the request. This request took no account of the existing demands on the SOCO – if the incident was in his area, he received the call. Consequently he often had to manage several calls at a time; he had no way of knowing when he would be able to visit the latest scene because there is no standard time in which to complete all the tasks at a scene; furthermore he had no means of contacting the victim to keep him informed of his likely time of arrival. When the SOCO eventually arrived at the scene he was often criticised for the delay, to which he would reply, 'Don't blame me, it's the system.'

These examples of the failure to provide the services expected by people are unfortunately not isolated incidents. Crime victims can be left feeling that it is as difficult to contact the officer responsible for their case as it is to identify the offender. If we had a problem with a newly-installed gas fitting, would we expect British Gas to insist on us identifying the fitter before they would take action? If we lost our baggage on a flight, would we expect the airline to tell us to contact the baggage handler? The answer is clearly 'no'. Important points are identified by these examples:

1   Police forces seem to be organised to provide a series of individual tasks rather than a complete service.
2   Police forces seem to structure work for individuals to perform without co-ordinating these efforts into teams engaged in delivering the whole service.
3   Police forces do not have quality assurance systems to identify shortfalls in the total service.

Individual tasks not complete services   The police response to a house burglary provides an illustration of this point. The police will undertake a number of discrete tasks. The call will be despatched by the control room to a constable, irrespective of the other calls he has been assigned. The constable will attend the scene as soon as he can, even if this means leaving another incident without completing all the tasks. At the scene he may be called away, or he may rush to complete it to attend another waiting call. The crime report will be submitted to the supervisor who will check it for administrative errors and then pass it to the clerk for processing. Once processed it will pass to the CID for investigation. Each task is a discrete entity; no one is accountable for the overall delivery of the burglary service. If the customer needs help or information, their first task is to identify who is accountable for delivering that piece of the service.

Individuals not teams The problem of accountability is complicated further by the existence of multiple objectives which may conflict with each other, or at least reduce the quality of service. The control room's objective is to despatch calls as quickly as possible because they believe they are being judged by their response time for the handling of calls. The officer receiving the call believes he is under constant pressure; therefore it is in his interests to deal with incidents as quickly as possible to enable him to be ready for the next call. His objective is to handle incidents as fast as possible. The sergeant relies on the crime report submitted by the constable to judge the quality of the service provided to the victim; therefore his objective is to ensure correct paperwork because he believes his supervisors will judge his supervisory skills on the quality of this paperwork. The clerk's job is to process the report; his role does not include a customer service. Finally the detective receives the report; his task is to catch the offenders – the victim's needs are someone else's responsibility.

Quality assurance The effectiveness of the investigation, judged by the detection of the offenders, and the quality of service to the victim, judged by the meeting of his expectations, depend on all the staff involved in the process. One of the striking features about the cases illustrated above is the extent to which individuals completed their tasks but failed to meet the needs of the victim or customer. In Case B, the individuals did everything they were expected to do, with the exception of keeping the victim informed. Unless there is a coherent service structure and a member of staff is accountable for monitoring the whole service delivery process, including quality assurance, the problems illustrated by the three cases will continue to occur. What is required is a radically different approach to delivering police services. At the heart of this new approach will be a commitment to determine what the community expects which will form the basis of a system of defining service delivery standards open to quality assurance monitoring. Once the service delivery standards have been determined, systems and procedures will have to be structured to treat the service as a whole, not a collection of individual tasks.

Future Perspective

In October 1990, the Association of Chief Police Officers (ACPO) published a strategic policy document, *Setting the Standards for Policing: Meeting Community Expectations.*[2] The document had been prepared by a working party with members from the Police Federation, the Police Superintendents Association, HM Inspectorate and the Home Office. The policy document has been the catalyst for developing the quality of service initiatives. There is a danger, however, of the document being misinterpreted, and of 'quality of service' being bolted onto existing systems of service delivery without consideration of the meaning of quality of service and why the current services are not meeting the standards.

Quality is not an absolute; it is a perception and it is relative. Passengers in the economy class on an aircraft do not expect the same standards as those enjoyed on the same aircraft by first-class travellers. However the airline must maintain the expected level of service for economy passengers to prevent them from complaining or taking their business elsewhere. Thus the quality of economy travel is relative, but cannot fall below a perceived level of expectation. This reality is recognised in the International Quality Assurance Management System Standard, the ISO 9000 series, which defines quality as 'fitness for purpose'. Quality under this definition responds to commercial needs by being realistic and commercially viable; in fact it recognises the requirements and expectations of the customer. The ACPO strategic document reflects this very concept. Police forces should not engage in a process driven by an abstract definition of quality of service. The driving force should be the meeting of community expectations, providing services which satisfy the public's needs.

Quality is an integral part of a structured and disciplined approach to management. It is not something which can be achieved by issuing an instruction and then continuing business as usual. The continuing theme of this book is the application of rational techniques to management within a structured and disciplined framework. The first step in the process is for the Chief Constable to provide a vision as to where the force should be in the future. There has to be a sense of direction.

The next step is to determine the current position of the force, as judged against the vision. Without this comparison it is impossible to determine what has to change and how. Implicit in this step is the determination of community expectations. Following the fact-finding stage, plans are made and implemented to achieve the vision. Day-to-day quality assurance and corporate evaluation provide information to tune the process and respond to external change. The entire process is cyclical, enabling the force to learn from its experience and to improve performance in response to community needs and a changing world.

Book Structure

As a practical guide to improving performance, the book is structured to take the reader through six stages of development, from basic concepts to maintaining commitment to improved performance. Each stage builds on the preceding stages.

Stage 1   Basic Concepts

Chapter 2 describes the concepts which provide the foundation of the structured and disciplined approach to management. The theme is the role of the manager as a problem solver. The objective is to prevent the premature imposition of solutions as the typical response to policing problems. Analysis and planning are the precursor to action. Chapter 3 describes the 'ideal police organisation' to provide a vision and context for the development process the book recommends. Without understanding the ideal it is impossible to make sense of the need for or the benefits of change.

Stage 2   From Concepts to Action

In Chapter 4 the concepts described in Chapters 2 and 3 are applied to the process of starting to move the police force forward to meet community expectations. The vision of the Chief Constable is translated into the corporate plan and goals to be achieved in the short term. This chapter establishes the structure for the development process.

Stage 3   Fact Finding

This stage emphasises the importance of understanding the current performance of the force from the perspective of the culture and management style (Chapter 5), the expectations of the community (Chapter 6) and the systems and organisation of staff (Chapter 7).

Although for the purpose of analysis the three elements have been separated, in reality they are interdependent. The fact-finding exercise will establish that the failure to meet community expectations is as much a consequence of poor systems and leadership as of a lack of commitment by individual members of staff.

Stage 4   Meeting Community Expectations

The information which has been collected in the fact-finding stage is the resource on which the future development will be built. The process of analysis has to be undertaken in the same structured and disciplined manner as the collection process. The complexity of the issues that will be identified require careful co-ordination and a wide range of staff being involved in developing options for change.

Stage 5   Community Problem Solving

The analysis in Stage 4 will identify the need to conceive of police services as meeting the needs of direct customers, those who generally receive a service in response to a request, and of indirect customers, who expect the police to control crime and maintain public tranquillity. Service standards for the direct requests for police services can be documented in service profiles, but the concept of service standards for indirect service is more difficult to define. In response to this difficulty the service is embraced in the term 'community problem solving'. The police meet community expectations through developing tactics to resolve those persistent social problems which adversely affect the quality of life in neighbourhoods. Community problem solving is based on identifying quality of life issues raised by the community. These problems are then subjected to a rigorous analysis, leading to the setting of sub-divisional objectives (Chapter 9), which is followed by action planning, described in Chapter 10. Chapter 11 describes how the results of police action are measured and made known to the community.

Stage 6   Maintaining the Commitment

Providing police services which meet community expectations is not a 'one-off' event; it is a continuing commitment to standards which can be shown to be linked to what the public need from the police. The structured and disciplined approach to developing the police force to achieve the mission must continue to be applied to monitoring performance and corporate planning. The final chapter emphasises this point by describing a process of corporate evaluation.

Notes

1   L. J. Scarman, *The Brixton Disorders 10–12 April 1981*. London: HMSO, Cmnd 8427 (1981).
2   M. J. Hirst, *Setting the Standards for Policing: Meeting Community Expectations*, London: Association of Chief Police Officers (1990).

2 Basic Concepts: Managing for Results

There is a tendency for police leaders to have an inward-looking perspective when it comes to measuring performance. The use of crime figures, road accident rates and the solving of major crimes do have a role to play in measuring the results achieved by police forces. However these measures are rarely linked to the fundamental criterion of police performance. At its simplest, a police force has to be judged by the extent to which it is meeting community expectations. The key questions for the Chief Constable are:

1 What does the community in my force area expect the police to achieve for it?
2 To what extent is the police force satisfying those expectations?
3 If there are no reliable measures of community expectations and the extent to which the force is satisfying them, how can the force be sure of maintaining public confidence?

Having established the meeting of community expectations as the fundamental performance criterion, the Chief Constable has to consider how he can achieve the mission of the force by improving operational effectiveness by making the best use of the resources allocated to him. Improvements in performance will not be achieved or sustained by chance; they have to be developed and supported within a management framework. To achieve results the management framework has to have a structure and discipline which retain sufficient flexibility to create an environment where staff can be creative and use their full potential. Without structure there is no consistency or sense of shared directions, but without flexibility innovation and imagination will be suppressed. People do not join police forces to be rude or lazy; such traits are the results of poor leadership. Even the most committed staff will find it difficult to maintain standards

13

if they are overworked, have no sense of a corporate purpose or can see no means of measuring the results they achieve.

This chapter is concerned with establishing some basic concepts of rational management by describing an approach to the identification and analysis of problems and a cyclical process of management to move from the planning stage through to the evaluation of results.

The key points of this chapter are:

1 To understand that effective management practice in the police is a system of problem solving.
2 To recognise the constituent elements of the process of problem identification.
3 To understand the elements of the management cycle.
4 To be able to apply the concepts of rational management to policing methods.

The Problem Identification Process

If the world was orderly, predictable and friendly then the need for managers could be challenged because employees would only need to be supervised within existing policy. Unfortunately the world of police work is far from orderly; it tends to be unpredictable and can be very unfriendly. Thus the manager's role is to take the world as he finds it and try to bring some order and predictability to his responsibilities. As he surveys his responsibilities he can identify those matters which are operating smoothly and do not demand his immediate attention. He will also identify areas where he must take steps to improve performance. There has to be a reason to change, either to remedy a current shortfall in performance or to anticipate the decline in performance and to take pre-emptive action. Therefore a problem in this context is defined as *the gap between the current state and some desired state*.

Problem solving is a complex process which starts with a careful examination of the issues to derive as much information as possible about the problem. The problem identification process is based on a series of simple questions:

1 What is the problem?
2 What is causing it?
3 Who is responsible for solving it?
4 What will show the problem has been solved?

5 What will happen if no action is taken?
6 Should the problem be redefined?

The process of analysis starts with a written description of what is known about the problem, including the reasons which make it a problem. Using this description the process will then apply the questions.

1 What is the Problem?

Having described the problem the first step is to establish the source. This may sound relatively simple, but it is one of the most difficult steps. It has often been said that 'not having enough manpower is the problem'. A lack of manpower can never be a problem; it can only be a symptom. If the public are concerned about an increase in the number of incidents of disorder in a particular neighbourhood, an option might be the deployment of additional patrols. If these are not available, the lack of patrols does not become the problem; the rising number of incidents of disorder is still the problem. Similarly a lack of overtime, police cars or equipment can never be problems; they may be constraints upon the options available, but that is not the same as being a problem. In the context of meeting community expectations, a problem is the difference between the ideal state of their neighbourhood as perceived by the community and the current undesirable state. The police have a role to play in meeting community expectations by improving the neighbourhood. In the first step in the process, the people experiencing the problem are identified. This will enable the process to be focused.

2 What is Causing the Problem?

There is a tendency to jump to conclusions about what is causing the problem. This must be avoided. Without exploring and documenting all facets of the problem, opportunities to identify solutions may be lost. In Chapter 11, an example is provided to show the need to analyse all the information about house burglaries to identify patterns which can then be the basis on which police tactics will be built. The analysis identifies two distinct types of burglary, to counter which different tactics are needed. Unless this information is fully explored, the full causes of the problem will not be apparent. As part of this same process, the people experiencing the problem should also be identified. The process of exploring the causes assists in the identification of potential indicators to measure the extent to which the problem has been solved.

3   Who is Responsible for Solving the Problem?

The manager must establish if he has a responsibility for solving the problem. There has been a tendency in recent years to assume that the police have a responsibility to solve all kinds of social problems. The Home Office have cautioned Chief Constables about extending their boundaries and assuming the responsibility for matters outside their traditional role (Home Office Circular 114/1983, paragraph 11). Thus before proceeding the manager must be confident that he has a responsibility to commit resources to solve the problem. The issues raised by this point concern what is sometimes called the mission of the organisation. In simple terms all organisations, including the police, have a mission or purpose. The founders of modern policing, Rowan and Mayne, laid down the police mission in 1829, with their instructions to the Metropolitan Police. Over the years the purpose of the police has become extended to include being a friend to those in need (Royal Commission on the Police, 1962). However a manager should ensure that he does not stray beyond the purpose of the force which is set out within existing policy. The questions concerning the mission of police forces in the last decade of the twentieth century will be discussed in Chapter 3. At this point it is important to note the need to have a framework of purpose within which priorities are identified and decisions made.

4   What Will Show the Problem Has Been Solved?

There is little point setting out to solve a problem if there are no means of establishing the results which have been achieved. The development of performance measures was raised in the paragraph exploring the causes. A manager should establish at an early stage the means he will use to satisfy himself that the situation has improved as a result of the actions he may take.

5   What Will Happen if No Action is Taken?

Having completed the analysis, it is good practice to consider the problem in the context of all the competing demands on resources. A manager must always have the concept of priorities at the forefront of his mind. He will not have sufficient resources to address every problem which may arise and therefore he will have to make decisions concerning those problems to which he will commit resources. Before he makes the decision he will have to establish the consequences of doing nothing in response to a problem. Where he believes he can live with the implications of doing nothing, he can use his valuable resources elsewhere. The structure process of identifying the causes of the problem and the extent to which it is a police matter allows the question of priorities to be answered with more confidence.

6 Should the Problem be Redefined?

The information obtained through the analysis will give a greater understanding of the nature, extent and causes of the problem. In the light of this information, the original definition of the problem should be reconsidered and amended if necessary.

These problem identification steps will be used as the foundation of the next stage, which is the progress towards considering options for actions to solve the problem. The structure and discipline of the problem-identification process must continue to be applied in the process of problem solving. The management cycle satisfies this need.

The Management Cycle

To proceed from the definition of a problem to its solution requires a system of management to transform ideas into actions. There are four distinct stages in this process:

1 The problem will be identified through the system of analysis. When the definition has been clarified the planning process will explore alternative methods of achieving the desired results and the most appropriate will be chosen.
2 The human resources will be organised on the basis of the plan.
3 When the preparations have been completed the plan will be implemented.
4 After implementation, the work of the staff will be monitored and controlled to ensure they understand their role and instructions. At predetermined points the results will be evaluated on the basis of the performance measures developed in the planning stage.

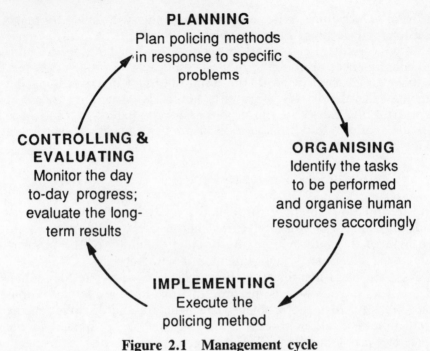

PLANNING
Plan policing methods
in response to specific
problems

ORGANISING
Identify the tasks
to be performed
and organise human
resources accordingly

IMPLEMENTING
Execute the
policing method

**CONTROLLING &
EVALUATING**
Monitor the day
to-day progress;
evaluate the long-
term results

Figure 2.1 Management cycle

Once the management process has moved through the four stages, the results of the evaluation are available to be used in the planning stage of the next management cycle. Thus the process continues as a cycle, where the lessons of the past are used to improve future performance. The elements of the cycle are shown in Figure 2.1.

Planning

The planning stage starts with an examination of the 'here and now' in the context of the established purpose of the force and follows the problem-identification exercise to the point where the issue to be addressed is defined in a form from which performance targets can be identified. When the existing performance of the force has been established, alternative policing methods can be explored to seek improvements. All the alternatives should be examined to identify their positive and negative aspects and then the most suitable method can be chosen. It is not sufficient simply to choose the preferred method, it has to be described in detail – identifying the components, the sequencing of these parts and the resources which will be required. Finally the monitoring and evaluation system and the performance measures have to be established.

The basic elements of the planning stage are shown in Table 2.1. It is worth remembering that it takes far less resources to plan a policing method than it does to execute it. Therefore time spent in planning is well invested because it should reduce the chances of operational staff wasting their time on poorly-designed policing methods.

Table 2.1   Planning

1   Establish and define the mission of the force.
2   Identify a vision of the future desired state of the force.
3   Obtain information and assess the present performance of the force in respect of the mission and thereby establish the gap between the current state and the desired state.
4   Explore options to improve performance.
5   Review each option to determine costs, advantages and disadvantages.
6   Identify the preferred options.
7   Transform the outline option into a specific strategy, identifying the major elements, their sequence and costs in staff and other resources.
8   Identify the performance indicators to be used, the means by which they will be measured, and the timing of these measures.
9   Determine the mechanisms for monitoring the progress of the strategy, anticipate variations and deviations from the strategy, establish methods for modifying the method when necessary.

Organising

To organise appropriate manpower it is necessary to examine the policing method in more detail in order to identify the various tasks and their constituent elements. Performance measures will be established to monitor the work of individual staff. Task analysis will be used to determine the relationship between tasks in order to construct job descriptions for individual posts. Task analysis will also facilitate the location of posts within an organisational structure, thereby establishing formal relationships between individual posts with specific responsibilities, accountability and authority. Finally task analysis is a critical ingredient in determining the knowledge, skills and aptitudes necessary for postholders to perform their work. These three matters follow in sequence, but the vital role of the task analysis is to link directly the policing method to the human resources that will execute the plan.

• Before leaving the organising phase, consideration must be given to the allocation of resources. It is unlikely that all resources will be made available for every project to be undertaken by the force and therefore some compromise has to be established on how limited resources will be shared amongst the force.

The key points in the organising process are summarised in Table 2.2.

Table 2.2   Organising

1   Identify from the methods the various tasks to be performed, analyse their constituent elements and establish performance criteria for each post.
2   Determine the relationship between tasks and construct job descriptions for individual posts.
3   Locate posts within an organisational structure, establish formal relationships between posts, including responsibilities, accountability and authorities.
4   Identify the knowledge, skills and attitudes necessary to perform the tasks to the predetermined criteria.
5   Establish the basis on which the resources will be allocated.

Implementing

The implementation phase can be seen in two distinct parts. First, there is the completion of preparatory stages which involves all the personnel who will be responsible for executing the strategy. Second, there is the actual execution of the method accompanied by monitoring and co-ordination of the tasks being performed.

The first step will be to appoint staff to fill the posts identified during the organising phase. By using the information gained during the task analysis, the training needs of individual postholders will be identified, and a training and development programme will be conducted to prepare the staff for their new roles. During this preparation phase a wise manager will ensure his staff are fully aware of what is expected of them as individuals and, in collaboration with them, he will identify mutually agreed performance objectives for individual posts. In addition the postholders must be given clear instruction which enable them to understand their responsibilities, to whom they are accountable and the extent of their authority. When the preparation has been c᷍᷍pleted the strategy will be initiated.

A major weakness of police management in the past has been a failure to co-ordinate and monitor policing methods. An integral part of the implementation and execution strategy is to make sure that the tasks are monitored and co-ordinated. The constituent elements of the implementation process are summarised in Table 2.3.

Table 2.3   Implementing

1   Appoint persons to fill posts.
2   Identify postholders' training needs and implement a training/ development programme to prepare postholders.
3   Establish and agree, in co-operation with individuals, their own performance objectives.
4   Formally assign responsibilities, accountability and authorities to postholders.
5   Initiate tasks to be performed.
6   Monitor and co-ordinate the tasks being performed.

Controlling and Evaluating

The monitoring and co-ordinating which is an integral part of the process of implementation can be seen as the basis of the tactical or day-to-day evaluation. The controlling which is an important part of the manager's responsibilities involves measuring the achievements of his staff against the targets which have been set. Changes may need to be made to tune the method to keep it on course. In the longer term the overall results will be measured in the corporate evaluation. The process of evaluation should be seen as an exercise which provides opportunities for the force and individuals to learn from their experience. The force must know what has been achieved in the pursuit of the targets and its contribution to improving performance. Individuals must also have the opportunity to know what they have achieved during the process. In appropriate cases the achievements of individuals should be formally recognised.

The final step in this phase is the submission of a formal progress report. It will be processed through an established review procedure to enable the lessons learnt in the first cycle to be included in the deliberations that will take place before the next management cycle is initiated. The constituent elements of the controlling and evaluation stage are summarised in Table 2.4.

Table 2.4   Controlling and Evaluating

1   Measure overall achievements in relation to desired results.
2   Identify reasons for results achieved and/or lack of achievement.
3   Assess the achievements of individuals against the predetermined performance criteria.
4   Make modifications to the strategy in the light of the evaluation results.
5   Recognise the contributions made by individuals and give appropriate rewards.
6   Submit progress reports on the established planning process for consideration in the next management cycle.

A Management Case Study: Unit Beat Policing

The value of adopting a structured and disciplined approach to management can be illustrated by describing how Unit Beat Policing (UBP) was introduced. The concept was sound, but the implementation weak. The results did not match expectations or the full potential of the system.

The Working Party on Operational Efficiency and Management which reported in 1967[1] established three aims for its review of police operational organisation. These aims were 'to find ways of providing a better service to the public, to increase the interest and responsibility of the man on the beat and to achieve more economic utilisation of manpower' (paragraph 6). They conducted a review of existing police operations throughout England and Wales. It was concluded that there was a general inflexibility in the methods of deploying uniformed police officers and that this worked against improvements in effectiveness and efficiency. They also identified a trend of increasing workload and either static or decreasing manpower.

The Working Party believed Chief Constables should examine the ways in which they used their officers in an effort to improve the service the public were receiving from the police. Having identified the problem and established performance goals, they went on to consider alternative methods of policing and, in an appendix to their report, they described a number of variations in uniformed police deployment. The most radical innovation in police deployment was found in the Unit Beat Policing concept implemented in Accrington, Lancashire. The Working Party urged Chief Constables to examine this method of policing to determine if it was relevant for adoption in other parts of England and Wales. The report was at pains to point out that it was not recommending the universal and immediate abandonment of the existing beat policing systems but was asking chief officers to review their own situation and performance in the context of a changing world. Whilst striking this cautionary note, the Working Party examined the Unit Beat Policing concept in a manner which would do justice to the planning steps set out in Table 2.1.

The goals of Unit Beat Policing were identified as follows: improving the service to the public by providing a faster response to their calls; improving public relations through closer contact with the community; a systematic collation and rapid retrieval of information to enhance crime detection; improved morale for constables to be achieved by a process of job enrichment; and increasing police productivity by satisfying increased workload demands with no increase in manpower. A strategy to implement Unit Beat Policing was contained within the Working Party report and included a job description for the area constable and a proposed organisational structure based upon a basic beat unit.

In hindsight, a critical deficiency in the Working Party report was its failure to identify key performance indicators. The report established with some care the problems the Unit Beat Policing System was designed to resolve, but it did not identify the means by which the achievement of the required results could be objectively established. The absence of performance indicators was further exacerbated by the Working Party's failure to place the Unit Beat Policing concept within a management strategy which contained a controlling and evaluating mechanism for long-term assessment.

The Working Party recognised the implications for officers when Unit Beat Policing was adopted. They were very specific concerning the duties and responsibilities of the area constable, to the extent that they published a job description for this post. They also recognised that the introduction of this policing system would radically alter the role and tasks performed by the patrol sergeant. The Working Party believed the sergeant would become a *leader and organiser* under Unit Beat Policing rather than merely a *supervisor*, as he had been in the past. Unfortunately they did not expand their ideas on this issue and, furthermore, there was no recognition of the radical change that would occur in practice in relation to the sergeant's role owing to the introduction of the personal radio. When Unit Beat Policing was introduced the patrol sergeant remained responsible for the activities of constables on the street, but with the simultaneous introduction of personal radios it was the person operating the radio control, the controller, who had the most immediate knowledge of the activities of the constable. It was the controller who directly supervised and deployed those officers to incidents and it was to the controller that requests for advice and guidance on operational matters were directed in the first instance. This tended to undermine the position of the patrol sergeant and make his role somewhat ambiguous in the new structure. This ambiguity was exacerbated when the post of controller was held by a constable. With the passage of time, a new role has tended to develop for the patrol sergeant, a role which involves a significant proportion of office work, as he is required to check and submit paperwork generated by the ever-increasing workload of constables on the street. If a thorough task analysis had been conducted before Unit Beat Policing was adopted, these problems might have been identified and resolved through the normal organisational process.

There were many other issues that arose in relation to the organising and staffing of Unit Beat Policing, not least of them the role of the CID. Detective constables were given specific responsibilities under the Unit Beat Policing Model but, in a review report published some years after the introduction of the system, it was stated that the role of the CID could not be assessed as it had not been possible to find an example of the detective constable being involved in Unit Beat Policing to the extent envisaged in the original design.

Despite the warnings of the Working Party that Unit Beat Policing should be seen as only one possible alternative for improving police effectiveness and efficiency, the concept was universally embraced by Chief Constables in the late 1960s. Some experimentation took place on a small scale in a number of forces, but generally Unit Beat Policing was imposed with the minimum of preparation for the majority of officers, almost no consultation and explanation and with no clearly specified objectives or performance measures.

The failure to identify performance measures made the final phase in the management cycle impossible: it was not possible to control and evaluate the performance of individual officers or the force as a whole if there were no benchmarks by which to judge performance. Thus formal evaluation formed no part of the management process of Unit Beat Policing. It is true that the original model has been modified significantly in many forces, but the exact reasons for these modifications and the consequences are not readily identifiable. In the absence of appropriate evaluative mechanisms, it is reasonable to say that the present form of uniformed patrol deployment in operation in England and Wales has evolved through some form of random selection based upon a rather vague notion of the management process. The changes have not generally occurred through an objective assessment of problems, performance measures and systematic evaluation.

Have we learned from history or will we repeat the mistakes of the past? In recent years new systems of policing have been adopted in many parts of England and Wales. These innovations have generally been known as community policing and it is not the purpose here to review in depth the management of these new methods.[2] This book does not promote one form of policing against another, but is primarily concerned with identifying and meeting community expectations by improving the effectiveness and efficiency of police forces through the systematic application of managerial concepts to all policing problems, no matter where or for what reason they arise. The central issue in police management is not to examine *the activities performed* by police officers but to ask what *results* are being achieved and whether these results constitute a better police service for the community.

Notes

1 Home Office, *Police Manpower, Equipment and Efficiency*, Reports of Three Working Parties, London: HMSO (1967).
2 M. Weatheritt, 'Community Policing: Does It Work and How Do We Know? A Review of Research' in T. Bennett (ed.), *The Future of Policing*, Cambridge: Cropwood Conference Series No. 15 (1983).

3 Basic Concepts: The Ideal Police Organisation

Chapter 2 described the fundamental elements of management based on the concept of identifying and solving problems. By using a very simple cyclical process, it was argued, a police force could move progressively from its current state to a more effective service. The ideal state would be one in which the community has complete satisfaction with the services the police provide. The chapter illustrated the concepts in a case study examination of the introduction of Unit Beat Policing. This chapter is concerned with developing the theme by describing an ideal police organisation in terms of the principles on which it is organised and does its work. To provide a context it is worth examining some of the basic leadership issues which seem to be relevant.

There has been a reluctance by Chief Constables and other officers of high rank to recognise the necessity of seeing police forces as organisations which are fundamentally no different from any other enterprise or business. Arising from this basic error there has been a tendency to hide behind the complexity of policing as a means of excusing poor management and leadership. The Home Office circular 114/1983 set the agenda for improvements in operational effectiveness and efficiency but, as the Audit Commission report number 8 showed, the impact in real terms has been remarkably limited.[1] This is not because it is not possible to improve police management or measure police effectiveness; it is simply because there are serious shortcomings in police management style, vision and leadership. A noticeable change has been seen in the number of police forces which set annual objectives and support them with some form of rational management system, but the extent to which police forces can demonstrate that they have improved the quality of life for their communities is very limited. Confidence in the police is unlikely to increase as long as the police seem to be consistently failing, or at the very least unable to measure the extent of their success.

The current debate inside and outside the service demonstrates the extent to which fundamental questions are being raised about the purpose of the police, how they are organised, and the extent and quality of the services delivered. Implicit in these questions are other issues which concern the extent to which the staff of police forces are able to respond to these challenges in the absence of leadership and organisational structures and procedures.

The key points of this chapter are:

1   To understand the need for all staff to share a sense of common mission and to have a vision of the future.
2   The need to have a culture and management style which creates opportunities for staff to achieve the mission.
3   To identify those factors which influence the culture and management style.
4   To understand the concepts of core police services and community problem solving.
5   To understand how the concept of policing by objectives can provide a rational framework to make management effective.

A Sense of Mission

What is police work trying to achieve? There should be a vision and understanding shared by all staff about the purpose of their work. The police have come to realise, in common with many other businesses, that they have to respond to the expectations of their customers if they are to be effective. Thus the shared sense of mission will increasingly be related to the meeting of community expectations. This is a fundamental issue for policing in the last decade of the twentieth century. The evidence of public perceptions of the police shows that it would be dangerous to assume that police forces have some intuitive understanding of what the public expects without the need to engage in conscious efforts to document this information. The police are not alone in this quest to satisfy customers, but when police policy makers turn to case studies from business, such as the turnround in the fortunes of British Airways as a result of their 'putting the customer first' programme, they should not lose sight of the basic business principles.[2] British Airways may have achieved an edge over the competition for customers in air travel by making those customers feel good about the friendly, smiling staff, but those same customers expected British Airways to take them to their destination safely. This simple fact must not escape the attention of the police policy makers. There is certainly a need to improve the confidence of the public by an overt commitment to ensuring services meet community expectations, but the public also expect to have an operationally effective police service.

Leadership

To achieve a sense of shared mission there has to be positive leadership from the Chief Constable. Leadership will create an atmosphere of excitement in which staff will want to achieve their full potential. Leadership is not sufficient on its own. It must be accompanied by a system of management which channels this energy and commitment into achieving results. Management systems are not ends in themselves; they are means to an end. The Chief Constable has to ask himself, 'Am I simply running a busy force, or am I leading and managing a force which gets results consistent with the mission?' Unfortunately the evidence from the Audit Commission report suggests there are more police forces which fit the former description than fit the latter. Without a conscious commitment to developing a community problem solving organisation, police forces will continue to be prisoners of the 'tail-chasing' system of management, unable to say where they are now or where they want to be in the future.

In Chapter 2, a system of rational management was described which involved a cycle of four phases: planning, organising, implementing, and controlling and evaluating. These basic concepts have been developed into a tiered process which is described as 'policing by objectives' (PBO). At the outset it is essential to see PBO, not as an end in itself, but as a process by which operational policing can be made more effective and the results can be measured. Ironically, at a time when the police have achieved significant improvements in operational effectiveness and reductions in real costs, the public are losing confidence in them. The police have been unable to demonstrate these improvements because they do not use a disciplined and structured management system. Experience and the seat of the pants no longer constitute a sufficient range of skills to meet the challenge.

Police work and police organisations require a sensitive and flexible approach to solving problems. The discretionary nature of police work and the diversity of policing problems encourage the use of a system which allows the greatest possible freedom to operational officers. However the legal accountability of Chief Constables requires that the freedom of operational officers be exercised within strict parameters. PBO is a management system which satisfies these needs and provides a framework within which sustained organisation development and improvement can be achieved.[3]

Policing by objectives was developed by Val Lubans and James Edgar following a review of the use of Management by Objectives by police forces in the United States. The principles and definitions used to describe PBO in this text are directly attributable to those authors.

Culture and Management Style

Policing by objectives as a system of management can exist in police forces which have different cultures and styles. Unless the culture and management style is conducive to the needs of a problem-solving system such as PBO, the results achieved will fall short of the full potential of the force. The culture and management style which is most likely to achieve results consistent with the mission will have the following characteristics:

1   The force is committed to devolving decision making to the point in the organisation closest to the problem to be solved. This is the concept of local action to meet local needs.
2   The basic command unit will be defined as the sub-division. Within this sub-division there will be a broad framework which assigns officers and civilian staff to primary functions, but there will be discretion given to the superintendent to vary this deployment provided standards of service are maintained.
3   Community problems are identified through a system of active consultation and solutions are developed in partnership with the community.
4   The sub-division has open systems of communication involving all staff who are encouraged to participate in the process of meeting community expectations and improving operational effectiveness.
5   The sub-division has a system which allows information collected in the normal course of delivering services to be collated and analysed to identify community problems. This system uses formal problem identification and analysis techniques to present issues to the sub-divisional management team.
6   The sub-division has access to the corporate policy-making pro-

cess. Policy issues are passed to the policy advisory group and from there to the chief officer group for ratification. These tiers provide a framework for 'bottom-up' and 'top-down' communications.

7 Headquarters departments have a formal mandate which is the support of sub-divisions in their efforts to meet community expectations. Policy decisions by headquarters departments reflect the force mission. Headquarters departments are held accountable to sub-divisions for the service they provide in support of sub-divisions through agreed performance and service standards.

Where a police force does not fit this broad management philosophy it should consider the implications in service delivery terms of these differences. For example, in a force with a highly centralised decision-making philosophy, how can superintendents be held accountable for the quality of service their sub-divisions deliver?

The culture and management style has an all-embracing influence on the way staff feel about their work and the force. How often are staff really consulted about the nature of their work, about how they feel it could be improved; and what is their understanding of the mission? This consultation has to go beyond meetings and newssheets. There is a need formally to measure the culture and style of the force and to determine the attitudes and perceptions of staff. This information is critical in determining the internal processes of improving the quality of services. It also provides senior management with a measure of their skills in getting commitment and understanding from their staff. Where the organisational culture and climate is found to have the potential to inhibit developments, changes must be introduced and their impact measured by resurveying the staff.

Ethical Standards

In addition to the management system's influence on the perceptions and attitudes of staff, there are other influences which can be described as the ethical and philosophical principles of the force. The foundation of these principles can be found in the oath of allegiance and the Statement of Common Purpose.[4] In some cases these principles are reinforced by legislation, as with the treatment of detained people which is controlled by the Police and Criminal Evidence Act 1984. To show overt commitment to these ethical and philosophical principles, police forces should have policy statements which set standards and principles in such matters as equal opportunities for employment and promotion, commitments to vulnerable minorities which may require special consideration, and the treatment of particular categories of victims, such as women who are raped or children who are sexually abused.

Boundaries of Responsibility

A third element which will influence the staff's perception of their work will be the extent to which they feel they are accountable for specific social problems. The Chief Constable has the responsibility of defining boundaries of accountability for his staff. For example, the task 'to prevent crime' is concerned with reducing opportunities for crime to take place and the general deterrence afforded by law enforcement activities, the so-called secondary and tertiary areas of crime prevention. The police have far less responsibility for the primary areas of crime prevention, such as welfare provisions, housing, education and employment. Therefore there is a need for the police to have policy statements related, but subordinate, to the mission statement, describing the boundaries of their responsibilities. In the absence of a clear definition of responsibilities staff will become frustrated if they feel they are being held accountable for the solving of problems over which they can exercise no influence.

Standards of Service

Every police force will say that it is busy, but few will be able to articulate with any precision what constitute their core services. Without this clear definition, how can there be any confidence that the service is meeting community expectations? Consider a simple example, such as the lost and found property service. A young man loses his wallet and reports the fact to the police station in the city. Later that night he receives a telephone call from the person who has found the wallet. He asks the person to take the wallet to the police station in the city because he lives some distance away.

The next day, in his school lunch hour, he walks the mile to the police station to collect his wallet. When he arrives, the enquiry office clerk says she cannot return his wallet because the sergeant who has the key to the store is having his lunch. The young man walks back to school empty-handed and returns after school to the police station. If the police force fails to define what constitutes the 'Found Property Service' from the customer's point of view, then there is a real danger that the service will be found wanting. Such a standard of service is unlikely to encourage people to have confidence in the commitment of the police force to the mission of meeting community expectations.

The example of the young man attempting to retrieve his wallet illustrates how procedures can defeat the mission of meeting community expectations. When the sergeant was given the responsibility for the security of the found property store, was the question of service delivery considered, or was the only concern the internal rules of the force relating to security? On a larger scale, most police forces will have systems of crime management, but how many of them were developed following an objective measurement of what victims of various categories of crimes expected or needed from the police? Once again there is the potential danger of conceiving police work as something the police 'do to the community' rather than as a response to clearly-defined community needs and expectations. The pursuit of the mission to meet community expectations requires an analysis of all structures and procedures to answer the question, 'Is this the best way of doing police work to meet community expectations?' If the answer is 'yes', then there is no reason to change, but if it is 'no', the implications have to be considered.

Irrespective of the community in which people live, they will expect the police to investigate the crime they report, attend a road accident in which they are involved and play a part in controlling crime generally. However the extent to which they are concerned if they do not see a patrolling officer from one week to the next in their neighbourhood, or become particularly anxious about the possibility of having their house burgled, will depend to a significant degree on where they live. Some communities place greater demands on the police than others because of the perceived problems of damage to property, theft and burglary, and the general quality of life in the neighbourhood, affected by such things as run-down properties, litter, abandoned cars and so forth. As a rule, where a community perceives its quality of life to be low, the people tend to make higher demands of the police to solve the problems which are believed to be the cause.

The diversity of these demands suggests that the police have two distinct groups of customers: those who make a direct request for police service or are the subject of police-initiated actions and the 'customers' who expect the police to maintain order in their community as a continuing commitment. The former group are in fact a minority of the population; the vast majority of the customers of the police have complex expectations concerned with the quality of their lives. In some cases the fact that they call the police may be a recognition of the police failing to meet their expectations of an orderly life. Thus the majority of police customers have a continuing expectation of the police as community problem solvers.

For the sake of clarity it is proposed to consider police services in two categories. First there are the direct services which are typically provided to individuals and usually as a response to a request from an individual. The second category could be termed indirect services; these form part of a coherent strategy to improve the quality of life for communities. The distinction is somewhat artificial because the tactics adopted as part of the indirect services may involve delivering services to individuals. However it is essential to make the distinction to enable problems to be analysed and solutions to be determined. The essence of the approach to community problem solving is the application of rational systems of management.

Core Police Services

The mission informs and instructs staff on the fundamental purpose of their work, but there is a need to provide a focus on precisely what has to be done. The first area of detail is definition of the basic services provided by the force; these have been called 'the core services' because they represent the direct 'business as usual' services to the public. They include categories such as (1) responding to calls for assistance and advice; (2) the investigation of crime; and (3) public services such as handling lost and found property. General and routine police work has to be categorised within core services to provide a framework within which standards of service can be defined. The process of auditing these core services to produce service standards is described later in Chapter 6. It is possible that the audit will raise fundamental questions about the services in the light of public expectations; consequently there may be a radical reappraisal of the range and content of the services in the future, but for practical reasons there has to be a starting-point.

Unless this exercise is undertaken and standards are defined, it is impossible to determine whether the service the public is receiving in response to a call, or in the investigation of a crime, is better or worse than it was last week, last month or last year. Declining standards will only be 'visible' when some crisis of confidence occurs. If there are no standards, how can staff be held accountable for quality of service, managers make decisions on the deployment of resources, and the public be reassured that quality matters? Where no standards have been set, senior managers take strategic decisions without being able to make any objective assessment of the impact on the service delivered by their staff. This is management by abdication or chance.

Community Problem Solving

To a degree the distinction between core services and community problem solving is artificial, but if the perceived complexity of police work has been a factor which has inhibited the quality of management in the past, anything which simplifies the issues must be useful. The basic process of delivering community problem solving is similar to that of core services. The police should adopt techniques to determine public needs and the anxieties of specific communities or neighbourhoods. What problems of crime, disorder and road safety are reducing their quality of life? This information is an integral part of the problem identification and analysis process. In responding to community expectations the police have a wide discretion in terms of the extent to which they respond on their own, the extent to which they work in a multi-agency response, and the amount of resources which are deployed. This is the classic context in which the system of setting annual goals, to be supported by sub-divisional objectives and action plans, should be applied. Policing by objectives is perhaps the most powerful community problem-solving process.

Community Consultation

If there is no understanding of the extent to which the force is meeting community expectations and no vision of the future, there is likely to be little change, except for the worse. But if there is a commitment to meet community expectations and this represents the vision of the future, then the whole process of change will be directed towards this mission. A key element will be the extent and quality of consultation with the community. The community will increasingly become a resource through customer surveys and broader-based consultation in residents' groups and so forth. The vision of the future will depend on the results of this consultation.

The consultation process must increasingly become a two-way process, with the results of police actions being passed back to individuals and groups to give visible proof of the commitment to serving their needs. This process will also provide opportunities to enlist the support of the community in partnership initiatives to reduce crime and improve their quality of life. Every opportunity should be taken to market the service. For example, where officers detect speeding motorists when acting in response to local concern about road safety, they should inform the motorist reported for offences of the reasons behind the action being taken. Hostilities can be suppressed and, even where the person is unhappy about being reported, he has the opportunity to see that the police are working for the common good and not just taking arbitrary action. This day-to-day consultation is all part of the image- and confidence-building process.

Policing by Objectives: A Summary

The first part of the chapter has described the factors which affect the way people feel about their work in police forces and the need for positive leadership and an ethical foundation. This is the human side of the enterprise, but if services of a high standard are to be delivered and community problems solved, it is essential to have a disciplined and structured framework to manage the process.

Policing by objectives (PBO) provides a management structure which is sufficiently disciplined to improve effectiveness but is also flexible, to create the optimum culture and management style to ensure staff achieve their full potential. The planning stage is usually the most comprehensive and time consuming as it involves a detailed review and assessment of the present performance of the force. This is the process described in Chapter 4, which discusses corporate planning. The corporate plan documents the current performance and sets targets for future development. In the next stage, step 2, the corporate plan is refined into specific goals which define the force-wide priorities; in step 3, objectives are defined, followed by action plans in step 4. Implementation takes place in step 5, and evaluation in step 6. The process is illustrated in Figure 3.1.

PBO is a systematic approach to management in which every element has a specific function to achieve a specific result and, although the model is extremely flexible, the underlying rationale and purpose of each constituent element should not be changed. If and when alterations are made they should be carefully considered in relation to the model as a whole, as a single structural change could significantly reduce its effectiveness. The principles of the concept should remain unchanged and true to the central purpose: to

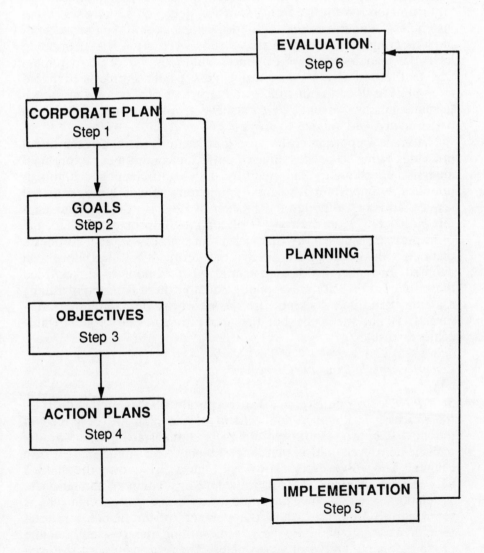

Figure 3.1 Basic PBO cycle

ensure that action plans on the street are a response to the corporate plan established by the Chief Constable.

When policing by objectives was introduced into Britain in the mid-1980s, it was directed primarily towards improving operational policing through the setting of what were often termed 'policing priorities', which were then reflected in sub-divisional objectives. Unfortunately, as the Audit Commission documents, there was often insufficient understanding and discipline about the process of implementing the system, so that results were often less than could have been achieved. This evidence reinforces the need to remain true to the underlying principles. Unless a police force is prepared to commit itself to the discipline and structure of a rational approach to management it is unlikely to achieve significant improvements in performance and service to the public. ·

The most important difference that the introduction of rational processes brings to police management is the commitment to problem analysis and planning. The need to analyse problems and plan solutions is as important for support functions as it is for operational service delivery. Although the concept of PBO is examined in Chapters 9, 10 and 11, in the context of community problem solving, the principles are implicit in the fact-finding processes and corporate planning. In some police forces the term 'PBO' has not been adopted. In reality it does not matter what name is used, provided the principles of PBO are applied. Equally, there is no point calling a system PBO if it does not use the necessary discipline and structure. It is not the name but the application of the process which achieves results.

Overview of Policing by Objectives

Step 1   The corporate plan   The corporate plan is at the heart of the process. The nature and content of the plan are described in the next chapter. The corporate plan is the starting-point of the management cycle and is therefore subject to an annual review and change. The PBO cycle shown in Figure 3.1 shows the linking between the elements as the process develops within an annual cycle. To elaborate and explain the context in which the corporate plan is set, Figure 3.2 illustrates how the elements of the planning process form a pyramid, with the peak representing the mission and the broad base any number of action plans. The important message from the diagrammatic representation is the path that can be tracked either from the mission to actions on the street, or from the actions of individual members of staff back to the mission. When staff are enabled to see this linkage, they are more likely to understand why and what they are doing, and become committed to a shared sense of mission.

Whilst the corporate plan may change from year to year, the mission and the culture and style will endure longer and be subject to little or no change. In a sense they represent the vision which is described in the mission and the underlying philosophical and ethical values of the police force. The corporate plan takes the mission as the benchmark against which to answer the questions, 'Where are we now?' and 'What needs to be done to get closer to the mission?' The starting-point is to pose the questions in turn to each of the core services. During the process of developing the corporate plan, measures of achievement and the role of the support services will be identified.

The answers to these questions will be based on the needs and expectations of the public. The corporate plan, although the ultimate responsibility of the Chief Constable, is a document which articulates the vision of a police force in tune with its community's needs.

Step 2 Goals When Step 1 is complete, the force has a clear statement of the current performance and the issues which seem to be inhibiting the full potential to satisfy community expectations. The corporate plan provides the basis on which priorities for action can be determined. This is the overall plan, and Steps 2 to 4, through a refining process, translate general policy into specific actions to achieve the overall result. Goals are the first stage in this process, and their purpose is to co-ordinate the efforts of all sections of the force towards achieving the results which are required by the corporate plan.

Sub-divisional and departmental commanders and managers have the responsibility to prepare provisional goals based upon their own problems and priorities. These provisional goals will be prepared after an examination and analysis of the particular problems facing sub-divisions or departments, as related to matters contained in the corporate plan. When the provisional goals are submitted to the policy advisory group they will be accompanied by a narrative description of the reason for each goal.

The policy advisory group will review the provisional goals submitted. Areas of common interest, overlap of responsibilities, demands for specialist resources, information needs and training requirements

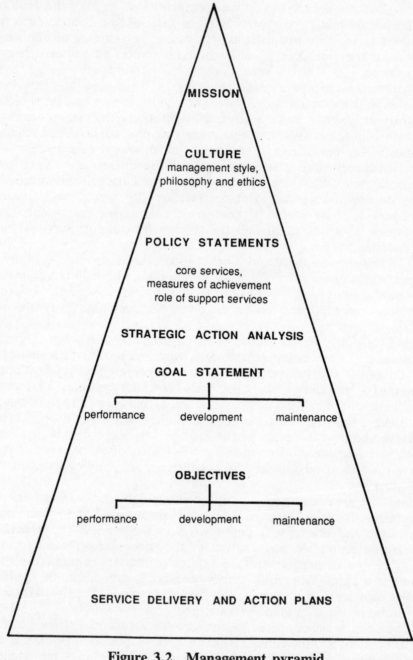

Figure 3.2 Management pyramid

will be identified. During this review the goal statement for the force will be agreed by the policy advisory group. The goal statement will then be prepared, containing a narrative description of the reasons for individual goals, thus providing a greater understanding of the priorities to be pursued at the objectives setting stage.

Step 3 Objectives The central purpose of goals is to provide a framework for force-wide co-ordination of effort and resources. Therefore goals will always be formulated as a result of an analysis of real problems which affect specific parts of the force. However they will be published in a form which makes them generally applicable throughout the force. It is in the process of setting objectives that the particular concerns of a sub-division or department come to the fore. The goals provide the basis on which the detailed analysis of the problems facing the sub-division is conducted by the person responsible for setting objectives. The majority of objectives will be set by sub-divisional superintendents, who will consult with their officers when the force goals are published.

Step 4 Action plans During the process of formulating objectives it is recommended that provisional action plans be prepared, as this process allows staff to consider possible courses of action in a practical and realistic way. Abstract plans which cannot be implemented in the real world are not helpful. A considerable degree of flexibility is envisaged in this part of the process, but it is recommended that some written record of action plans be maintained. This will assist in establishing which of the provisional action plans are actually used, and with what success.

Step 5 Implementation In many respects the implementation of action plans will not radically alter the activities which staff are already performing: PBO is not a magic solution to crime and public disorder. However the force will become more concerned with the reasons for staff carrying out these activities and the results they produce. The enforcement of road traffic legislation will not be done for the sake of it; rather it will be part of an action plan designed to 'reduce road accidents' or 'reduce complaints from the public about speeding vehicles' or 'reduce the annoyance caused by illegally parked cars near a bingo hall'. Furthermore the activities of several officers will be co-ordinated towards the same results, and the impact of these actions monitored and evaluated. It must not be forgotten that all the other police activities – servicing calls from the public, attending court, maintaining public order at football matches and so forth – will be continuing as before.

Step 6   Evaluation   It might be argued by some that action planning does not represent a radical innovation in police management. If there is some validity for such an observation concerning action planning, the same cannot be said for evaluation. It is in the area of evaluating results that police management is most vulnerable, and this part of the PBO model does represent significant innovation.

The process of setting action plans involves a requirement to monitor the results achieved from their implementation; thus evaluation is a continuous process in one form or another. The degree of evaluation on the sub-division will be a matter for the sub-division, but it should not become an end in itself. In the first instance, a force review will be conducted after the first year of operation. This will involve the submission of an evaluation report from sub-divisions to divisional commanders, who will produce a composite report covering their division for submission to headquarters. This review will form the basis on which the next cycle in the PBO process will be formulated.

Organisation Development

The fact-finding exercise which must precede the preparation of the corporate plan should make a distinction between the operational issues and organisation and management development. The management process which follows the publication of the corporate plan reinforces the distinction by separating performance goals, which concern operational improvements, and development goals, which draw attention to the need to improve management support, organisation procedures and so forth. Both performance and development goals will follow the basic management cycle (Figure 2.1) but, in the case of development goals, there may be no reason to specify objectives and action plans. Consider the introduction of word processing to sub-divisions to improve the productivity of existing typists. The implementation will follow an existing force procedure and therefore the identification of intermediate steps in the form of objectives and action plans would be superfluous. The result will be achieved when the equipment is installed and put into use; therefore the outcome measure is obvious. The rationale for introducing the equipment was based on a need to improve the productivity of existing typing staff to reduce the amount of typing done by police officers. In these circumstances a performance goal could be defined concerning a reduction in man hours spent by police officers in typing and clerical work. Objectives and action plans should be produced for this goal because it will be the responsibility of the sub-division to evaluate the contribution made by the equipment towards improving use of time. In most cases headquarters departments will have the responsibility for implementing actions in response to development goals, but operational officers will evaluate the organisational and management improvements which may be achieved. This distinction is important. Just as community relations activities cannot be assumed to be successful without direct evaluation by the public, neither can changes made in the support provided by headquarters be assumed to be successful without direct evaluation by operational staff.

Co-ordination

The integrated nature of PBO is an essential factor in its successful implementation. Unless the structure and discipline of the underlying rationale becomes the accepted management process, the benefits will be only partial. The commitment to the process is as important in the framing of sub-divisional action plans as it is in the development of the corporate plan. Consequently someone must be accountable for ensuring that the process is maintained and developed. Ideally this should be the person who is responsible for producing the corporate plan. The importance of the corporate plan cannot be overstated and therefore a chief officer should oversee the corporate planning process, having responsibility for presenting the plan to the chief officer group for approval. The department which provides the assistance in the planning function should have the responsibility for the day-to-day co-ordination of the PBO process. These responsibilities will include:

1 Publishing and disseminating the corporate plan and goal statement.
2 Providing a consultancy service to assist in the implementation and development of the management process.
3 Maintaining a record of development plans and objectives.
4 Acting as a focal point and index of best practice for action plans.
5 Monitoring, on an agreed schedule, the results of development plans and objectives.
6 Receiving annual evaluation reports to prepare the corporate evaluation.

7   Collating the information to draft the corporate plan for the coming year.

Concluding Comments

This chapter and the preceding one have been concerned with setting out some basic concepts about management systems and the human side of organisations. The purpose has been to establish a context and to describe the framework which will be used to indicate in later chapters how police forces can respond to the challenges of the last decade of the twentieth century. To use an analogy, the canvas has been prepared for the picture to be painted. The next chapter is the start of that process. The Chief Constable has accepted that there are reasons for change and the change must take place in a structured and disciplined manner.

Notes

1   The Audit Commission Police Paper Number 8, *Effective Policing – Performance Review in Police Forces* (1990).
2   A. Campbell, M. Devine and D. Young, *A Sense of Mission*, London: The Economist Books Ltd (1990).
3   V. A. Lubans and J. M. Edgar, *Policing By Objectives*, Hartford, Conn: The Social Development Corporation (1979).
4   M. J. Hirst, *ACPO Strategic Policy Document, Setting the Standard for Policing: Meeting Community Expectations*, London: Association of Chief Police Officers (1990).

4 From Concepts to Action: Making a Start

An effective police force will have the following:

1 A vision of the future shared by all the staff.
2 Positive leadership within a culture and management style which encourages staff to achieve their full potential.
3 An understanding of community needs and expectations supported by objective evidence.
4 Defined standards of service supported by a quality assurance system.
5 A commitment to improving the quality of life in the community.
6 A commitment to a structured and disciplined system of management.

This profile describes the essence of the ideal police force, and therefore is the goal to be achieved. The profile provides benchmarks against which the Chief Constable can judge the performance of his own force. Current evidence supports the observation that no force meets these criteria and therefore there is a need to change. It is the process of initiating this change which is the subject of this chapter.

The key points of the chapter can be summarised as follows:

1 Identifying the importance of balancing demands with resources within a framework of defined standards of service.
2 Identifying benefits to the key participants in police services.
3 Describing in outline, the process of gaining commitment.
4 Understanding the role of the corporate plan and the constituent elements.
5 Identifying the need for a framework to co-ordinate the process.

Identifying the Issues and Thinking About Change

Chapter 3 was concerned with principles and concepts. This chapter is concerned with the initial process of translating those ideas into action and results. Before accepting the need to change there has to be a reason – a perceived or measured failure to meet the service standards expected by the public. The validity of the reason must be examined by the Chief Constable. If he is not convinced there is a need for change, he is unlikely to be able to convince others of the need. This process of analysis is perhaps assisted by asking a series of questions, and using the answers to identify the issues and draw some conclusions about the need for change: Is there a problem? Does it matter? If so, what are the negative consequences? Who suffers?

In the previous chapters comments have been made about the pressures and challenges to which present-day police forces are subject. The heart of the problem is the relationship between the public and the operational police staff. If the quality of service declines, the public loses confidence in the police; this is reflected in criticism, which in turn lowers the morale and commitment of police staff. The cycle starts again with a further decline in the quality of service. Add to this process the increase in demands on police forces, which are outstripping the allocation of resources, and the lack of vision in police leadership to tackle these fundamental issues. Paradoxically, because of the inadequate systems of relating performance to the quality of management and leadership, it is the lower levels of the service who have to take a disproportionate amount of the pressure. Put quite simply, the major casualties of inadequate management are the staff who are delivering the service and the public who receive it.

The resolution to this tension between demands and resources will depend on:

1 standards of service being defined;
2 resources being matched to service standards;
3 demands and standards being monitored and changes measured; and
4 rational decisions being made, if demands increase, on the choice between the allocation of additional resources or a reduction in the level of service.

In the absence of this rational framework the decisions which adjust resources to demands do not cease to be made. In reality it is the staff who are handling the day-to-day demands who are making the decisions. As a consequence the quality of service varies between sub-divisions, and between the individuals who are delivering the service. Highly-committed staff are likely to give a 'better' service than uncommitted staff, but who sets the standards, and who measures whether they are achieved?

The *problem* is a failure to meet public expectations; this occurs most often when staff do not know what are the standards of service required and resources are outstripped by demands. The *solution* is to meet public expectations by determining standards of service which can be achieved with the resources available. When this is achieved there are benefits for everyone:

The public – service delivery standards which reflect their expectations will be consistently achieved.

Staff delivering the service – they will know what is expected of them and how their performance will be judged. They will also know that they will not be expected constantly to balance demands and resources by cutting corners on service.

Senior officers – they will have an agreement broadly defining standards of service related to finite resources from the providers of those resources, a means of measuring the quality of service delivered and a rational framework within which to make decisions to balance demands against resources, or to seek any variation in the resources. They will also be in a position to hold their staff accountable for standards. At a time of financial restraint or cutbacks these benefits have added significance as they can form the basis of rational decision making when determining priorities.

The providers of the resources – they will have an opportunity to interpret the expectation of the public by providing resources to meet these service standards.

The same tensions exist between resources and the demands made on sub-divisions to solve community problems of disorder and quality of life. As the demand to meet standards in core services intensifies, there will inevitably be less scope to use resources to meet community problem solving expectations. Therefore, in determining core service standards and allocating resources, the calculation has to include some capacity to respond to these additional public expectations.

Even in the absence of other issues, the need to reduce the tension between demands and resources, and hence to begin the process of restoring public confidence, provides a powerful reason for change.

Getting a Contract with the Key Participants

The Chief Constable and his chief officer colleagues may be convinced of the need to change, but it is essential to gain commitment from key participants as a precursor to achieving commitment from all the staff.

Two questions which may be posed by staff have to be answered convincingly: first, 'Why should I give my commitment?' and second, 'I've heard this all before and nothing changed; what's different this time?' These questions serve as a useful basis on which to make the initial plan. The Chief Constable and his team accept the problem and see the solution as meeting community expectations. The product they are selling, however, is not quality of service, it is the opportunity to improve the working lives of their staff, a greater level of customer satisfaction and more accountability for service delivery to the police authority. In short, it is benefits not concepts. The initial plan must identify a means of convincing these three audiences that their commitment to the necessary changes will fulfil their expectations of a better world.

To respond to the second question, the plan must contain a convincing outline of practical steps which can be taken, with a realistic chance of achieving the benefits. The basic steps in the plan will be these:

1   Describe what will be different and why. The essential elements have been described above in the summary of the benefits to the public, police staff, senior officers and the providers of the resources. These can be elaborated to meet local circumstances.
2   Determine a plan to sell the benefits to the key participants. This plan should ensure that the message is delivered directly by the Chief Constable or one of his team to all levels of the force and the public through the police authority and consultative forums.
3   Describe the initial fact-finding mechanisms. The essential first step in the process will be to undertake the groundwork to answer the basic question, 'Where are we now?' The here and now applies equally to the need to determine the perceptions of staff about their work and the public's perception of police services. It is essential to measure the extent to which staff share a common view of the mission of the force and their attitude to

important factors which can affect their commitment to excellence in the service they provide. The diagnosis of service standards can be achieved by a comparison of public expectations with measures of current service levels. This process has to be sold to the various audiences in such a way that they can see that they will be involved. If this is not achieved the whole process could be stillborn. A process which is committed to determining public expectations must have convincing methods of identifying these expectations. This process will be described later as the service audit.

4 Establish tentative timescales to demonstrate a determination to make progress and deliver. In reality it may only be possible to place firm timescales on the service audit, but the implementation of the first phase of minimum service standards should be estimated.

5 Identify the person with the overall responsibility to co-ordinate the process and the resources that will be committed to meet the timescales. The co-ordinator must be a member of the Chief Constable's team to give the necessary overt commitment to succeed.

6 Determine a co-ordinating structure to oversee the various stages of the process. There is a need to involve the public, and this need is reflected at the management level. Inevitably levels of service will be a compromise between the desired and the possible, and therefore the process of achieving this compromise should involve some form of public participation. To reflect this need the management structures could involve some participation by members of the police authority.

This process of analysis and reflection has enabled the Chief Constable to identify the reasons for change and the benefits. There has also been an opportunity to consider the process of change and the means of achieving a commitment from the people who will be involved in making it happen. The next step is to start the process.

Making a Start

At some point the Chief Constable has to accept the consequences of making no changes or decide to respond to the challenge of meeting community expectations and measuring achievement. The first stage is to brief the top team and gain their acceptance of the benefits to be achieved by a change which will make meeting community expectations the mission of the force. The briefing should include opportunities for the benefits and disadvantages to be fully explored, emphasising how current problems could be relieved by the changes envisaged. For example, decisions on budget priorities are likely to be more objective if they are related to consequences for service delivery standards. An opportunity should be given for hidden difficulties, political considerations and any other issues which have to be considered to be raised. But, in the absence of a viable alternative, the central concept should only be modified, not rejected.

To demonstrate the commitment to change the force, the Chief Constable explains the rationale and the vision of the future in a statement of intent. The explanation must be based on some coherent structure which enables all participants to see in simple terms how the process will unfold and how the various elements are linked. The management pyramid shown in Figure 3.2 fulfils this function. The starting-point is the vision which will be based on a notion of the mission of the police force. It may not be possible, or even desirable, at the start to define the mission because it will evolve through the participation of the staff in the development process. However at a minimum the Chief Constable must define what he sees as the tentative mission. The next level down can be met by adopting the 'Statement of Common Purpose and Values' and summarising the basis on which it is proposed to manage the force in the future.[1] Key elements of this culture and management style were listed at the beginning of this chapter. Having described the vision of the future, the next step is to describe the process which will be used to achieve the vision. To underline the commitment to making progress the future should be documented in a corporate plan which will serve as the route map to guide the process.

The Corporate Plan

The force is embarking on a process of development to provide a police service which 'meets public expectations'. The corporate plan provides a reference point to guide the process towards achieving the ends described in the Chief Constable's statement of intent. The corporate plan is a dynamic document which will be subject to review and change each year. It is the base reference document for the development process, taking the force forward from the current state towards the future desired state, where public expectations will be met. For ease of reference and to assist in the annual process of review and amendment where necessary the following format is suggested:

Section I – the culture and style of the police force;
Section II – policy statements documenting core police services; measures of achievements; the role of support services;
Section III – the strategic action analysis, and
Section IV – goal statement.

Section I The Culture and Style of the Police Force

In addition to the ethical and philosophical principles on which the work is based, including such policies as equal opportunities, there is also an organisational culture which guides the relationships between members of staff and defines the expectations of different ranks, roles and posts. While all staff know it exists, it is surprising how much potential there is for confusion and, in fact, misinterpretation of expectations. Furthermore, at a time when changes are required to enable the force to meet community expectations, it is essential that the corporate plan documents the starting-point at which change can take place. If the starting-point is not clearly defined, how will the changes be identified? In this context it should be recognised that the documenting of the current management system does not deny opportunities to change any part, if a case can be made. The test will be: 'Is there a need to change any part of the system of management to move closer towards meeting public expectations?' Only if the answer is 'yes' should change be considered.

Existing documentation provides the broad outline which describes the culture and management style, but, as Chapter 5 will argue, there is also a need for positive steps to seek more information from staff at all levels. The purpose of such a survey is to try to identify those factors which are inhibiting staff from achieving their full potential in terms of both effectiveness and standards of service. These inhibiting factors can be seen under two headings: first, the extent to which there is a shared mission, and second, the extent to which the work environment encourages a sense of belonging, support and satisfaction.

Section II Policy Statements

One of the major constraints in determining service standards, and thereby measuring quality, is the rather vague definition of what the police actually deliver. When we talk about responding to the report of a burglary, what precisely constitutes the service? What are the police responsibilities to the victim and what is the responsibility of victims of crime support schemes? When we talk about traffic law enforcement, what are the primary objectives of the police actions? When we are clear about what constitutes police services, how will we measure success? The same types of questions can be asked of headquarters departments – what are their responsibilities for developing and supporting service delivery? These may seem to be basic and simple questions, but very few police forces will have defined their work in clearly-documented services with quality assurance measures and very few support functions will be able to produce, if requested, a mandate defining their contribution to the service delivery functions of the force. But, without these policy statements, how can rational and informed decisions be made about resource allocation? How can development plans be prioritised to ensure that those with the greatest pay-off are undertaken first? In this section of the corporate plan, core services are defined, measures of success are described and headquarters departments produce mandates which show their contribution to service delivery activities.

II (a) Core police services The purpose of defining core police services is to enable them to be analysed in terms of public expectations and as a consequence to have standards of service defined to monitor quality of service. The sub-division delivers a range of core police services such as:

1 Responding to calls for assistance from the public; this should not be construed as simply describing the receipt of calls and the dispatching of police officers. In fact it covers the whole range of activities which can be used when a person contacts the police at a time of personal crisis or simply to ask for advice. It may not involve a face-to-face contact with a member of the force.
2 Investigating crime; all reported crimes require a response, which will vary according to circumstances. The range of response options will be based on a combination of effective case management criteria and victim service standards.
3 Enforcing road traffic legislation; the enforcement of traffic legislation is based on the need to maintain an appropriate level of compliance with the legal controls on traffic, which enhances road safety and facilitates traffic flows.
4 Community problem solving; the first three core police services

are principally reactive; in addition there is a related area of police work which involves the resolution of the root cause of these individual demands. A simple example would be the nuisance caused by noisy young people on street corners or shopping areas. Individual complaints will receive a police response but the solution to the problem often has to be found in a more sophisticated approach, for example by the provision of alternative venues for the young people to congregate and socialise. Traffic hazards caused by parents collecting their children from school is another prime example of a situation where changing people's behaviour is the real solution to the problem. Community problem solving is approached by the application of rational systems of problem identification and action planning.

II (b) Measures of achievement The overriding measure of achievement is customer satisfaction – the extent to which the force is meeting community expectations. Inexorably linked to this measure is the extent to which the public are aware of, and have confidence in, the achievements. This is the marketing dimension of the service. Unless the public are made aware of the commitment to meeting their needs and have information which demonstrates the extent to which they are being met, their level of confidence will be unaffected. The core services represent the work priorities of the force, therefore they will be the principal basis on which the extent to which community expectations are being met will be measured. Levels of service for each core police service must be defined and systems established to monitor them.

The principal aim of the force will be to be an effective deliverer of services, but a subsidiary aim will be to give value for the public money invested. Therefore in meeting public expectations there will be a requirement to monitor costs and continually strive either to achieve more for the same investment or to actually reduce costs.

II (c) The role of support services The role of the parts of the force outside the sub-divisions is to support the achievement of the core services. In some cases, such as the Force Control Room, the support is operational, while in other cases, such as the Management Services Department, it is less directly involved, but still provides an important function as a facilitator of service delivery. However headquarters departments can be pulled between two competing priorities, the provision of agreed support functions and the development of initiatives or projects to improve operational policing or reduce costs.

By adopting the concept of core police services, the corporate plan provides a reference point upon which sub-divisions can build their work and measure their achievements. It is equally important for support functions to have a documented and agreed mandate, and an agreed means of measuring their achievements. Where departments are required to develop initiatives, undertake research or respond to some new requirements, there is a need for a mechanism to structure these projects and determine priorities and timescales. In the absence of such mechanisms there is no defined line of accountability or control to the corporate plan.

Section III   The Strategic Action Analysis

Up to this point, the corporate plan has described what exists and defined what should exist. For example, sub-divisions deliver the elements of the core police functions but there are no existing standards of service based on documented expressions of public expectations. This part of the corporate plan is concerned with identifying those gaps between the current state and the desired state – the vision.

Before examining the detail of the desired state, it is perhaps worth asking some basic questions about the way executive management feel about the current state. In essence, what is it that creates anxieties? What is it that challenges their sense of professional competence? What causes them to feel publicly vulnerable? If they were to be more content and less anxious, what would change? To document this part of the corporate plan, the Chief Constable and his team have to use their imagination and intuition and consult as widely as possible to identify those issues which are inhibiting the development of a police service committed to meeting community expectations. A productive method of undertaking the strategic analysis is to produce headings which identify a particular problem area and then to list in summary form the issues related to the problem. These problem areas will be linked directly to the policy statements which have been produced in the previous stage.

For example, when the question is posed, 'To what extent is the force currently meeting community expectations?' the following issues may be identified:

1   There is no objective evidence of the service the community expects.

2 There are no existing mechanisms for determining community expectations.
3 There is no objective internal or external system of determining priorities based on community expectations.
4 There are very limited mechanisms for measuring the achievement of public expectation.

In this era of financial constraint, anxieties may exist about the quality of existing financial planning and control, identifying specific issues such as the following: (1) financial planning is *ad hoc* and cannot be related to service delivery; (2) financial control lacks precision and does not provide sufficient support to strategic decision making; (3) current methods of financial planning and control are open to criticism; (4) service delivery is not costed.

The purpose of the analysis is to provide an agenda for the development process which will take the force from the current position to the desired state. The problem statements described in the strategic analysis form the foundation of the goals to be achieved in the next twelve months.

Section IV   Goal Statement

The final section of the corporate plan is concerned with identifying specific targets or goals to be achieved in the coming year. The process of setting goals is based on the strategic action analysis which has identified the extent to which, and the reasons why, the force is not achieving the ideals which have been defined in the policy statements. The solutions to these problems are then articulated as specific challenges to be overcome by a process of development, or improving operational effectiveness, or increasing public satisfaction.

In the first year of this process it may be necessary to develop the goals through a limited analysis of basic issues to enable a start to be made. In subsequent years the process should be made more sophisticated, to embrace a wider consultation with the community and internally with staff at all levels. The process will be described in detail in Chapter 8.

Co-ordinating the Process

By this stage the Chief Constable has said what is going to be done and why, and has supported the vision with a corporate plan. The challenge now is to deliver. The process should be co-ordinated by one person of chief officer rank. The Deputy Chief Constable, who has limited responsibilities on day-to-day issues, makes a suitable candidate for the task. Although the corporate plan gives the detailed direction and goals of the development process, there is a need to have a structure through which it will be co-ordinated and the results will be measured and marketed. The broad contents of the structure can be summarised as follows:

1   The objectives to be achieved in the short and medium term.
2   The timescales for the major elements in the process.
3   The resources to be committed, both full- and part-time.
4   The management structures.
5   The marketing process.

The development process will use the same concepts that have been described in Chapters 2 and 3. It is vital to base change on a sound foundation of knowledge and therefore there will be a major commitment to a fact-finding exercise. The audit of existing performance, procedures and systems will create a large number of staff who will become well informed about many of the key issues which will have to be considered in the development process. It is important to balance the range of the issues examined in the first phase of the fact-finding exercise against the need to deliver some tangible evidence of progress sooner rather than later.

The primary focus must be the services delivered, the customers and the staff delivering the services. The first phase of the fact-finding exercise will consider questions under three key headings:

1   *Culture and management style*
    What are the perceptions of staff about their work and the working environment?
    Do staff share the same perceptions of priorities?
    Is the current culture and management style creating opportunities for staff to achieve their full potential?
    Is there a consensus amongst staff about the style of policing?
2   *The service audit*
    What services are delivered?
    What are the existing service delivery standards?
    What are the systems used to monitor service delivery standards?
    What information provides the evidence of customer needs and expectations?

3 *Systems and procedures*
   Do systems and procedures facilitate the delivery of services?
   Are staff organised to enable them to make a full contribution
   to service delivery or support functions?
   Do staff understand their role and have the necessary skills and
   knowledge to undertake their work?

There are many other issues which could be listed but these are the
key areas. In the first phase it is important to keep the attention
fixed on the service delivered. When the fundamentals of identifying
core services with service standards and quality assurance systems
are in place, the horizon can be extended to include support services
and other equally important matters. However, until the force knows
what it is delivering and to what standards, other considerations are
side issues.
   Chapters 5, 6 and 7 will describe the fact-finding exercise based
on these three key areas. In Chapter 8, the process of analysing the
information will be described. The raw data which have been collected in the process will have to be prepared in a format which will
enable conclusions to be drawn. This work should be undertaken by
the team established by the Deputy Chief Constable as part of his
co-ordinating responsibilities. The information which is collected in
this process will challenge many of the existing systems and philo-
sophies; therefore it is essential that it should be made available to
as many members of staff as possible to enable them to bring their
experience and skills to bear on the development of solutions to the
problems it will identify. The use of working groups to make progress
on individual issues has many strengths and should be considered.
   Following this analysis the corporate plan will be reconsidered
and, where necessary, amended to take account of the new information. The development process will then be started, using a disciplined and structured approach to achieving goals. An outline of
the process is described in Figure 4.1. It will be a matter of local
circumstances determining how far and how fast the force will proceed in the short and medium term. These decisions will also determine the resources to be used.
   The co-ordination of the development process will also be tailored
to local conditions but some general considerations will apply in most
circumstances. Meeting community expectations does not absolve the
Chief Constable from his duty to oversee the operational responsibilities of the force – this is the guiding principle on which he makes
his decisions. In the process he will consult the other members of

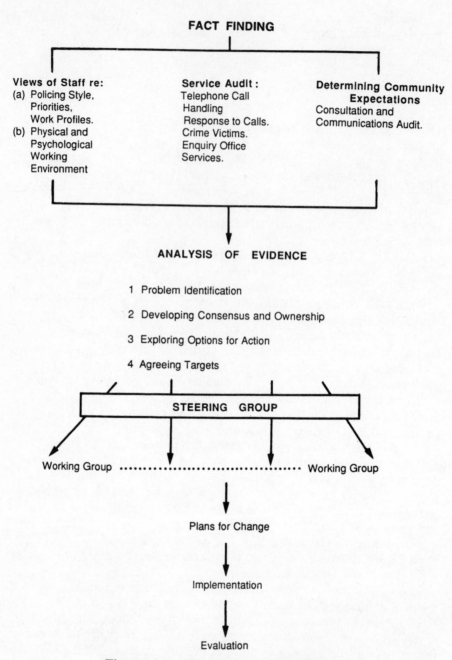

FACT FINDING

Views of Staff re:
(a) Policing Style,
    Priorities,
    Work Profiles.
(b) Physical and
    Psychological
    Working
    Environment

Service Audit :
Telephone Call
Handling
Response to Calls.
Crime Victims.
Enquiry Office
Services.

**Determining Community
Expectations**
Consultation and
Communications Audit.

ANALYSIS   OF   EVIDENCE

1 Problem Identification

2 Developing Consensus and Ownership

3 Exploring Options for Action

4 Agreeing Targets

STEERING   GROUP

Working Group .... Working Group

Plans for Change

Implementation

Evaluation

Figure 4.1   The development process

the tripartite arrangement; therefore the co-ordinating structures of the development and change process should include mechanisms to seek the views of the police authority and the inspectorate as Home Office representatives. The arrangements will vary from place to place. A sub-committee might be formed from the police authority to act as an advisory group, or a small number of people drawn from community groups, crime prevention panels and victims of crime support groups might be formed in a less formal structure as part of a steering group which would also include members of the force. This steering group would oversee the work of the core services working groups during the service audit phase and then later, in the implementation phase. The long-term role of the steering group might be to develop into a Quality Assurance Board, with the responsibility to monitor the achievement of the standards of service. Such a body would mirror consumer watch-dogs in other public and former public utilities, such as OFTEL, which oversees the telecommunications industry. The body would also demonstrate a continuing commitment to standards of service and openness by the police force.

Finally the marketing process will have to be carefully considered to ensure that the message reaches and is understood by all the key audiences. Senior managers at the superintendent level should be part of the marketing process. They should be fully briefed and also given the responsibility to take the message forward to line managers – the inspectors and sergeants. External audiences in the form of sub-divisional consultative committees, community representative bodies and the police authority must also be part of the marketing exercise. Some critical success factors will apply, no matter who is the audience:

1 Remember to sell the benefits, not an abstract concept – the 'what's in it for you' message.
2 Tailor the message to the particular audience.
3 Concentrate on the short-term benefits and timescales; this reduces the feeling that it will always be 'jam tomorrow'. When you are up to your waist in alligators, the promise of the swamp being drained at some future date is not very comforting in the short run.
4 Provide convincing evidence that the benefits are achievable and that there is a viable plan.
5 The final hurdle in the marketing process is to counter the 'we've heard it all before and nothing happened then' comment. It is

likely that this comment arose because there is past experience of people with the power who did not have the courage to make changes when their own opinions were challenged or when it would have required some change from them. A strategy to counter this potential ambush is to include in the message a recognition of the potential disadvantages and specifically those which may affect senior management. Having identified the issues, an undertaking can be made to respond positively, even if this means changing previous views, policies or management styles.

6 The style and messenger have to be determined. There is an important role for the Chief Constable in this initial selling exercise. The style of the presentation will depend on the audience. There is a danger of being too extravagant and raising initial expectation too high. The message has to contain all the essential points but also be practical and pragmatic in its approach.

Converting the vision into action and results will take time, but the quality of the final achievements will be significantly influenced by the quality and thoroughness of the initial preparation stages. As with any journey into unknown territory, the quality of preparation may be the difference between survival and oblivion.

Note

1 M. J. Hirst, *ACPO Strategic Policy Document, Setting the Standard for Policing: Meeting Community Expectations*, London: Association of Chief Police Officers (1990).

5   Fact Finding: The Culture and Management Style

The effectiveness and standards of service delivered by a police force depend on the commitment the staff have to the achievement of the mission and goals. This principle applies equally to the staff who are in the front line of service delivery and to those who perform supporting functions. Motivating staff and encouraging compliance with standards are fundamental management skills. The Hawthorne Experiments in the late 1920s demonstrated the apparent irrationality of men and women at work. It was found to be impossible to predict the productivity of workers by making variations to the workload, reward systems and the physical working environment. Observations of everyday life provide examples of the apparently perverse nature of human behaviour. A manager has to recognise the possibility of a non-rational response to his managerial plans and furthermore transform this apparent difficulty into a strength and benefit. In some circumstances it is possible for a committed workforce to continue to be effective despite inept management, but a poor manager should not count on this bonus indefinitely.

The problem of ensuring compliance with management policy is a common feature of all work situations and for the police there are special difficulties. A Chief Constable is able to make all kinds of administrative and bureaucratic rules, but it is far more difficult to control the standard of police service to the community. The constitutional independence of the office of constable severely restricts the force's ability to make rules which limit the exercise of a police officer's discretion in law enforcement activities. In addition to the theoretical legal limitations, the nature of policing on the streets makes close supervision of police work very difficult. The typical style of day-to-day quality assurance means that supervisors have to rely almost entirely upon the reports of their officers for their information about incidents. In many cases police officers are the sole source of such information and, even where two officers are present, a consensus description may emerge as to what has occurred. Peer and group solidarity are powerful features of the police occupational culture. The invisibility of police work to supervisors makes it particularly difficult to monitor and control. Unfortunately a common response by police managers is to introduce more administrative and bureaucratic rules. When this strategy apparently fails a typical response is to produce yet more rules and procedures, and it is this cycle which tends to increase the alienation of operational staff from their supervisors and create the illusion of control.

Although there is perhaps no absolute definition of the ideal characteristics of a police force committed to the delivery of excellent services, the following are some of the key success factors in creating an environment where staff can give their best.

1　The Chief Constable has an overt commitment to a mission and goals which is shared by all the staff.
2　The police force expresses a sense of commitment to high standards of service.
3　There is a recognition by managerial staff of the need for freedom of action and an understanding that mistakes honestly made should not be punished.
4　Quality assurance monitoring systems are imaginative and based on clear statements of expectation and delivery standards.
5　There is a supportive organisational system and culture which promotes self-development.

The key points of this chapter are:

1　To recognise the human dimensions of work and management.
2　To understand the practical limitations of managerial control in police work.
3　To be aware of the possibilities of conflict existing between staff who provide the services and staff with management responsibilities, and to appreciate the consequences of this conflict.
4　To recognise the need to have a management system which is appropriate to the needs of police work.
5　To recognise the need to have a management system which involves both 'top-down' and 'bottom-up' communications.
6　To understand the management issues associated with the perceived low status of the uniformed constable.
7　To understand the need to be aware of the perceptions of staff

providing services about their priorities, importance of tasks and policing style.

8   Within the context of the culture and management style, to understand the influence of communications, decision making, the allocation of work, the integration of individuals and groups, the rewards system, and conflict and competition.

Police Officers' Attitudes to Work and Supervision

Applicants to the police service have attitudes and opinions which comprise their mental image of the police and police work. Police selection procedures stress the need for personal integrity, self-reliance and self-discipline on the premise that an integral part of police work is the need to think and act decisively, using individual initiative. Selection procedures endeavour to recruit officers with these qualities and training procedures seek to reinforce their importance. A questionnaire survey of police recruits suggested these procedures were relatively successful in selecting candidates with opinions which reflected these principles of police work. The questionnaire contained a number of statements concerning police work and the recruits were asked to respond on a four-point scale, indicating their agreement or disagreement. Between 66 and 90 per cent of the recruits agreed with the following statements:

'The tradition of the police service is based on individual action and responsibility.'
'In the final analysis, a police officer is personally responsible for his actions.'
'The more freedom of action that an officer has, the better he will be able to perform his work.'
'Police work experienced in practice is vastly different from the work that is described in the various orders and regulations.'
'Your past experiences are the best guides to your actions in most circumstances.'

The two latter statements suggested recruits anticipated placing reliance on past experience to guide their actions and saw orders and regulations as being less relevant to the real world. Two other statements were related to rewards within the force and perceptions of senior officers. Nine out of ten recruits believed that 'individual initiative was rewarded in the police' and 'senior officers were in touch with the needs of police officers on the ground'.

The same questionnaire was given to a group of police constables who had been serving for five or more years. Their opinions in respect of individual action and responsibility, the need for the freedom of action in order to be an effective police officer, and experience being a critical guide to decision making were identical to those expressed by the recruits. However less than 20 per cent believed individual initiative was rewarded in the police and only 14 per cent believed senior officers were in touch with the needs of police officers on the ground. The differences in the responses to these questions were quite remarkable, given the similarity of the responses to the other statements. The image these constables had of their own responsibilities and the requirements to be an effective police officer appeared to conflict with their perceptions of the rewards system of the force and their belief that senior officers did not understand operational police work.[1]

In another questionnaire survey, data were obtained from police constables as part of an evaluation study of changes in policing methods on the sub-division. Before the change in policing methods there was a group of ten constables who were known as permanent beat officers. Each officer had specific responsibility for a beat and was expected to be the link between the police and the community. To pursue this role they were given a considerable degree of freedom concerning the hours they worked and the specific activities they performed. During the experimental period these officers became part of a group of constables who were responsible for a much larger area. They tended to lose identity with their small section of the community. They were given responsibility for responding to calls from the public and were expected to investigate more than two-thirds of all the crimes reported on the sub-division. In short they changed from individuals who could plan and manage their activities according to their knowledge and the needs of the community, to being part of a group controlled by matters outside their influence. A comparison of the responses of the permanent beat officers to the questionnaire, before and one year after the implementation of the system, showed dramatic declines in their satisfaction with their freedom to choose their working methods, the amount of responsibility they were given, their opportunities to use their abilities, working relations between senior officers and constables, and the way in which the force was managed. These results clearly demonstrated that the experiment brought about a reduction in job satisfaction for the officers who took part. They also illustrated that management can change the level of job satisfaction experienced by constables through changes in the work environment.[2]

A third problem occurs when the staff providing the service do not share the definition of work priorities of their immediate supervisors. A research project examined the work of permanent beat officers who had the responsibility of providing the foot patrol presence in neighbourhoods being posted to beats on a continuing basis. The beat officers were asked to describe their usual work profile, which was then compared with the results of a survey of the sergeants and inspectors who were responsible for supervising them. In this latter survey, two work profiles were produced; in the first the sergeants and inspectors were asked to describe their understanding of the actual work profiles of the beat officers. This showed a fairly close relationship with the responses of the beat officers. In the second profile, the sergeants and inspectors were asked to define what they believed was the preferred work profile of the beat officers; in other words, to respond to the question, 'What do you think these officers ought to be doing?' This profile showed significant differences from the actual work being done. The differences were typified by the greater emphasis on law enforcement activities by the sergeants and inspectors, rather than community problem-solving work emphasised by the constables.[3]

It would be dangerous to exaggerate the significance of this evidence but it does point to some useful lessons. The first research evidence showed how management styles and the actual demands of the work conflicted. In the face of this conflict, constables were obliged to construe officers with command responsibilities as inept and lacking in knowledge and understanding. This view of command officers is hardly conducive to positive leadership which will encourage officers to follow new ideas and developments. Initiatives from the top are likely to be written off as another aberration of an out-of-touch leader.

The second research evidence showed the danger of imposing a new system of policing on officers who provide the service, without first understanding the strengths and benefits of the existing system. As a consequence of this failure to collect the facts and plan change, officers were implicitly required to limit, as far as possible, the damage to service delivery caused by a system of working imposed from the top. The lesson is clear: before any changes are made to service delivery systems, the current levels of service have to be determined and the staff involved in developing changes which are designed to improve the service. Anyone can impose a new system of policing if there is no need to consider the effects on service delivery. The final point from the research illustrates the potential for staff who are responsible for service delivery not to share a common view of priorities and, by implication, goals. Positive leadership is a critical success factor in all organisations. It is difficult to achieve, but will be impossible if staff and supervisors have different priorities.

Returning to the opening comments of the chapter, meeting the community's expectations by delivering services which reflect their perceptions of an excellent police service will only be achieved through positive leadership which will create motivated and committed staff, working to a shared mission. The research evidence has shown some of the potential problems in achieving this standard of management, therefore the process of developing improvements in police services should begin with an audit of the culture and management style. If the current leadership style creates a perception of incompetence, reduces the quality of service delivery, reduces job satisfaction and allows a lack of synchronisation between the priorities of staff delivering services and their supervisors, then any proposals to change are likely to be still-born.

Management Systems

The root of the alienation experienced by constables appears to be that operational officers, constables and, on occasions, some first-line supervisors, believe they have different objectives from their senior officers. The constables' orientation is towards the street police philosophy of action, relatively unimpeded discretion, with experience of the past as a guide for decision making. This is seen to conflict with the apparent objectives of senior officers of administrative orderliness and adherence to rules and procedures as ends in themselves. It is a conflict between the inherent risk taking of street policing with the ultra caution of the bureaucrat.[4] This alienation between the street police culture and senior officers appears to occur relatively soon after a recruit joins the force. In addition to the conflicting perceptions of leadership style between operational staff and senior management, there are also conflicts at the intermediate level, with sub-divisional management officers believing their effectiveness is inhibited by oppressive controls on their decision-making discretion by headquarters departments and chief officers.

Police organisations have had a tradition of centralised control with decision making the prerogative of the highest level. The development in recent years of larger police forces has had the effect of moving the authority for decision making further away from constables who perform the operational tasks. In many large police forces, operational officers have no apparent influence on the policy-making process and may rarely see the person who makes the decisions. It is interesting to note the comments made by a Royal Commission 60 years ago. At the time of their report, police forces were considerably smaller than they are today, but the Commission was concerned that, as police forces increased in size, the instructions issued to subordinate officers became more elaborate. This tendency to increase the issuing of rules arose in some cases

> from insufficient personal contact between subordinate ranks and their responsible chiefs and from the natural desire of the latter to shield themselves from blame for any mistakes on the part of their subordinates by the issue of instructions setting out the proper course to be followed in every foreseeable emergency. (Royal Commission on Police Powers and Procedure, 1929, paragraph 4).

It is impossible for remote, centralised decision making to reflect accurately needs of operational personnel; therefore staff who deliver the services tend to question the validity and competence of the centralised structure in achieving the goals of the police force.[5]

There appears to be strong evidence to support the conclusion that the management system of police forces is the reverse of what is required for the effective delivery of services, a point underlined in another context by the reports from the Audit Commission.[6] Police work demands a system which will encourage initiative, discretion and decision making and not a system which tends to inhibit or destroy these qualities. The police management style must seek to balance the need for an appropriate degree of control to maintain accountability with the greatest possible freedom of action and discretion for officers to plan and control their work. The key question for the audit of the culture and management style concerns the extent to which the style of leadership at all levels creates a working environment which encourages commitment and opportunities to deliver excellent services. In simple terms, police forces should develop a system of accountability that relies more on trust than fear.

The Perceptions of Role and Status of the Constable

A positive management style will develop an environment where the rules and practice match the actual needs of the work. Because the quality of police services depends on the ability of individuals to make decisions in the best interests of the unique needs of the individual 'customer', highly rigid and centralised rules and procedures will not assist in service delivery. A second critical factor is the perceived status of the staff responsible for delivering the front-line services – the uniformed constable. If the person delivering the services feels undervalued as an individual, he is less likely to regard the services he is delivering as valuable to the police force. The evidence from research has identified the apparent paradox between the espoused philosophy of the force, which asserts the primacy of the uniform beat function, and the reality of the treatment uniformed officers believe they receive. As a generalisation, the uniformed beat patrol section of the force contains the least experienced constables, sergeants and inspectors. It is the section to which specialists are returned for indiscretions or after disciplinary action. It is the section of the force from which manpower is taken to respond to short-term or even long-term resource needs elsewhere. Officers seeking promotion are encouraged to leave uniformed patrol work to become specialists. Most damaging of all, uniformed constables themselves tend to perceive their work, and consequently themselves, as having low status in the eyes of the rest of the force and the public.

Before a solution can be proposed, the nature of this problem must be identified. The importance of uniformed patrol work is not disputed; the difficulty appears to be the absence of a means of clearly establishing the achievements of the uniformed patrol force and the skills which are required for these activities. In our society, status is something which is given or acquired mainly through achievement.

A sense of personal worth is probably the most important factor which will determine the extent to which staff will deliver quality services. The achievement of this goal is inexorably linked to the other key issues which have to be addressed if a police service is seeking to meet community expectations. Therefore the issue is not 'how do we improve the status of the uniformed constable?'; it is the wider question of developing excellence in terms of service delivery. In fact the achievement of excellence will resolve the status issue. The challenge is to reverse the implications of the perceptions amongst uniformed constables that they are workers without job descriptions who believe they perform the residual tasks after everyone else has decided what they would prefer to do.

Key factors in reversing this perception are:

1 Defining service standards in a format which documents precisely what is required by the person delivering the service. Consequently the constable will know what he has to do and to what standard.

2 Monitoring the standards of service delivery and providing positive feedback to the constable, correcting behaviour that does not meet the standards and creating a sense of achievement when standards are met.

3 Measuring workloads against resources and linking these to service delivery standards. Simply allowing more and more work to be assigned to officers without recognising the implications for quality standards will signal a lack of commitment to excellence.

4 Establishing systems to reward achievements in skill levels. The scope to achieve this in the short term is constrained within Police Regulations, but attempts should be made to reward additional skills which are directly related to meeting community expectations through excellent service.[7]

The Culture and Management Style

'Culture and management style' may seem to be a somewhat pretentious term to describe the way people feel about working for a police force, but on reflection it does provide a real sense of the human side of work. The culture concerns the extent to which staff feel proud to be members of the police force, their sense of belonging to the corporate identity, the extent to which fear or trust is the predominant management ethic and their commitment to service. The management style influences the way they feel about their colleagues, the extent to which they feel valued as individuals and the confidence they have in the ability of their managers. Driven simply by self-interest, people are only obliged to work to a level above the threshold which prevents them from being disciplined. Fortunately applicants to police forces have a sense of service and commitment which motivates them to perform above the minimum threshold, but this commitment is not always sustained and, in many cases, the reasons can be found in the culture and management style. Unfortunately managers spend insufficient time seeking feedback on the current state of the culture and management style in their area of responsibility. When staff become less effective, all too often the reaction is to blame them, without considering the reasons, which may lie with the manager.

Another common, but mistaken assumption is to believe that the Chief Constable is the only person who can influence the culture and management style of the force. He undoubtedly has a significant influence on the way staff feel about their work, but everyone makes a contribution. The leader of a team can inspire and motivate his staff or suppress commitment and innovation. Staff can take a pride in their work and get things right first time, or they can do the minimum, secure in the hope that someone else will correct omissions. At a time when workloads are increasing, it should be the goal of every member of staff to produce work for colleagues which is of a high standard. In a survey of a broad cross-section of staff, only 3 per cent strongly agreed with the statement, 'When I receive work from colleagues it is always of a high standard.' Therefore, whilst the process of change to enable service delivery to meet the needs of the community requires strategic action, unless everyone accepts that they have a contribution to make to the working environment, success will at best be limited.

Because excellent services are only delivered by the conscious efforts of the staff, it makes sense to include, as one of the first steps in the process of developing the force to respond to the challenge of meeting community expectations, a fact-finding exercise to determine how staff feel about their work and their working environment. Community expectations will be met by a combination of professional competence and skill, and commitment at a personal level to the ethics and philosophy of service. The police force has to be organised, structured and led to create opportunities for staff to do their best. The fact-finding exercise must be designed to provide evidence on which the current state of the force can be assessed from the perspective of creating these opportunities for excellence. The information should be collected from two sources. The first of these is the staff who are responsible for direct service delivery, such as patrolling constables, enquiry office staff and detectives. The information will determine the perceptions of the staff delivering the services on such issues as the importance they attach to particular tasks, their perceptions of their supervisors' priorities and the balance between demands and available time. The second source of information is the opinions of all staff about a range of issues which combine to determine the way they feel about their work. The

purpose of both parts of the fact-finding exercise is to provide information on which the process of change, which will inevitably
accompany the process of meeting community expectations, can be
based. The development of standards for core services and the
restructuring of the force to meet these needs is the mechanistic
element of the change process. To achieve results the human dimensions have to have equal priority. It is the development of the human
issues which requires the extensive knowledge about the current
culture and management style which the fact-finding exercise is
designed to provide.

Survey of Service Delivery Staff

The purpose of this survey is to establish the attitudes and perceptions of the staff who have the primary responsibility of delivering
services. In an ideal world, their priorities will reflect the needs and
expectations of the community in which they work, they will feel
able to allocate sufficient time to deliver these services to the standards expected, and their perceptions of the appropriate style of
policing will be conducive to the meeting of community expectations.
The survey is designed as a diagnostic tool for the sub-division or
force to determine whether, or to what extent, the attitudes and
perceptions of these staff are at variance with the ideal.

The key questions will be:

1 What do they see as important in terms of their priorities, in
   relation to a range of offences and policing problems?
2 Do they think their immediate supervisors share these priorities?
3 In relation to a range of tasks, how do they rate them in terms
   of importance or see them as part of their job?
4 Do they feel they spend sufficient time on these tasks?
5 What are their perceptions of policing styles?

The definition of service delivery staff should include, in addition to
constables, staff such as those working in control rooms and station
enquiry desks, and the special constabulary. Although it may require
a considerable number of questionnaires to be processed, there is
great value to be gained by inviting all staff in these posts to take
part. In addition to collecting important information, the survey also
sends a powerful signal to these staff, underlining the extent to which
the force values their opinions. The survey can therefore be the first

step in developing a team approach to the changes which will be required to meet community expectations.

Survey of all Staff

The purpose of the survey of all staff is to provide an opportunity to obtain baseline data describing their opinions about factors which influence their attitudes to their work. This information can then be used to diagnose the current culture and management style and determine if there is a need for remedial action. A survey repeated after actions had been taken to improve the staff attitudes to work would measure any changes which had occurred. Finally the survey provides a very powerful symbol of the commitment of the Chief Constable to listening to his staff and being prepared to change in response. Where change is deemed necessary, it will be made towards improving the management of human relations issues to achieve a consensus and shared perceptions amongst staff of the mission, the means of achieving results, and an understanding by everybody of their own and others' contribution to the mission. Key concepts determining the degree of success or failure of achieving a coherent and integrated organisational approach will be the quality of communication and decision making, the means by which work is allocated, the extent of feelings of team work, the way people feel rewarded, and the management of conflict and competition. Each concept will be examined in turn to provide a definition, an explanation of its importance, and some examples of positive and negative aspects of its influence on the organisation.

Communication   Information can be considered the life-blood of the organisation, having a critical influence on the commitment of staff to a shared sense of mission. The communications systems are primarily concerned with disseminating information, but they perform many other functions which may not be obvious at first sight. For example, open communication systems are more effective in conveying information but they also demonstrate a commitment by the force to honesty and entrusting staff with knowledge. When people feel they are not being told something, they tend to look for reasons why, which may generate mistrust.

Communication methods should be (1) open and say what they mean, so that people trust the information and do not have to 'read between the lines' to get some hidden message; (2) flexible, with the communication methods changing to suit the information needs:

simple information can be transmitted on paper, but more complex matters use direct face-to-face contact; (3) responsive to the needs of the organisation – large organisations need to adopt methods which reflect their size and may differ significantly from those of smaller, less complex organisations.

Communications systems must be as effective from the bottom to the top as they are in passing information in the opposite direction. Systems with feedback loops will enable senior officers to test their staff's understanding of the instructions passed down. In the absence of this feedback it is dangerous to assume that staff have interpreted the instructions in the way the author intended. A second function of the feedback loop is to provide a means by which senior officers can use the knowledge and experience of staff in the development of ideas and initiatives. To obtain the maximum benefit from this upward communication the manager must have the confidence to allow his staff to be constructively critical. If he is not able to encourage this openness then he is only going to hear what his staff believe he wants to hear. If staff believe the person at the top only wants to hear good news, that is what he will always hear. The danger arises when the bad news eventually ambushes him.

The value of the 'top-down' and 'bottom-up' communication systems is obvious, but the need for communication between staff on the same level is equally important. If, for example, communications between area constables and detectives are poor, the information gathered by the former officers may not be available to the detectives and consequently crimes may remain undetected.

Good communications systems are not a luxury. When they are poor there is likely to be confusion amongst the staff as to their role and contribution towards achieving the goals. When confusion and uncertainty are the hallmarks of poor communication, the predominant means of information dissemination becomes rumour and speculation. An equally damaging consequence of poor communications from the bottom up will be the potential for strategic decisions to be made with incomplete information and mistaken beliefs about the true facts, and without the opportunity to consider the ideas of staff who are closest to the problem. As a consequence the manager becomes increasingly remote from the problems of the real world and his instructions can become unrealistic, damaging his credibility.

Decision making Decision making is the problem-prevention or -solving activity of management. When a problem occurs decisions have to be made and the choice to ignore the problem actually means that the decision is made by default. In the organisational context, decisions are made for the purpose of directing the efforts of individuals towards achieving goals. Therefore the quality of those decisions will be significantly affected by the information which is available to the decision maker. Thus, as a guiding principle, decisions are best made closest to the problem and the source of the information. Unfortunately, with a centralised control and decision-making policy, the chance of the most appropriate decision being made is reduced as the problem is passed up.

An organisation with a good decision-making system will have clearly-defined policy and authority levels providing individuals with formal guidelines which clearly establish the boundaries of their responsibilities and accountability. Policy guidelines will recognise that the most appropriate place to make decisions is closest to the problem and the point in the organisation which has access to all relevant information. This ideal system has a number of implications for the organisation. The need to have access to information implies the need for appropriate communications systems where people are able to be open and honest with each other. If good communications systems do not exist both vertically and laterally then there are likely to be implications for the quality of the decisions made. Reward systems will be discussed later, but it is essential to recognise that the quality of the decision-making process will be significantly affected by the type of rewards system in operation. If the culture encourages and rewards risk taking amongst managers within preset policy, it will reduce the likelihood of managers abdicating their responsibilities and passing problems up through the organisation. Furthermore it will produce a culture in which managers will be able to develop and expand their skills and expertise.

Probably the most important aspect of organisational culture which will affect the quality of decision making is the degree of trust existing between managers and their staff. Staff should believe their managers can be trusted with information and will not use it against an individual. Supervisors should be willing to trust the judgement of individuals and accept that occasional mistakes are inevitable. In a climate of mutual trust not only will the decision-making process be more responsive and therefore of a better quality, but there will also be the opportunity for managers to learn and develop. To encourage commitment by all staff, the culture should enable officers of lower rank to contribute to the decision-making process. It is very easy for staff associations and trade unions to be critical of police management, but if they are to be involved in contributing to the decision-making process they must be constructive and provide alternative solutions to those they criticise.

Allocation of work   The allocation of work will have an important influence on the attitudes of staff to their work. The trend towards increasing specialisation of police tasks has been said to have reduced job satisfaction among uniformed officers by narrowing the scope of their work or by preventing them from taking an incident from the initial report through to its conclusion. Many of the issues are familiar to the social psychology of work in industry, where production line methods were claimed to have caused similar problems. Some reversal of the trend has been attempted recently, for example with the transfer of responsibility for the investigation of less serious crimes to the uniformed branch. However the issue is not whether to increase specialisation or to decrease it. The question for the manager is to establish the tasks which must be performed and then determine the people who are best qualified to undertake the work in the context of achieving service delivery standards. There is almost no likelihood of the job satisfaction of uniformed constables being enhanced by the transfer of a task which everyone believes is a wasteful use of resources. Constables who have been given the responsibility for the investigation of less serious crime may complain about the additional work, but they are also likely to feel more aggrieved about having to do a task which is very unproductive. In addition such work is not likely to be seen as valued and therefore it is hardly likely to inspire a commitment to excellence.

Decisions about the allocation of work will inevitably involve the consideration of tasks which can no longer be justified. Unfortunately there has been a tendency for police managers to restrict their response to increased workload to the annual demand for additional staff, without providing evidence of the consequences for service delivery standards. It will be argued in the next chapter that a powerful reason for developing definitions of service standards for a range of core services is to provide the basis on which resources can be matched to workload. Unless workload and resource reviews form a part of the annual planning cycle, staff are entitled to assume that their responsibility is simply to deal with volume, with effectiveness and quality relegated to second place. This review process should also consider the continuing value of tasks, because to continue to allow staff to perform redundant or inefficient tasks is one of the surest methods of reducing commitment to excellence and discrediting management competency.

Being part of the team   The principal reason for the organisation of resources is the need to combine the energies and skills of a number of people to achieve goals which would be unobtainable through the efforts of one individual. The statement may appear so obvious as to be unnecessary. Unfortunately one of the major factors inhibiting the improvement of productivity in organisations, and particularly the police, is the lack of co-ordination and integration of the efforts of individual officers and the various sections of the force. To a degree the nature of the work makes the sense of team work throughout the force difficult.

Individuals need to have an identity with others who perform the same tasks. Studies of the police have shown that small group membership is an important aspect of police work and particularly relevant to job satisfaction. Feeling part of a team provides an opportunity for learning the job and provides mutual support at times of difficulty or emotional stress. The manager must provide the circumstances in which a group identity can develop.

A sense of belonging to a group is important to individuals and is essential for the organisation. By belonging to a team, individuals are able to share a desire to achieve common objectives and share a common commitment to excellent standards, and thus their work is co-operative and co-ordinated. In complex organisations such as police forces, integration occurs on more than one level. Constables are members of small teams, such as a group of area constables or detectives. The next level is the sub-division and it is essential the various teams of officers also accept their membership of the larger team and share sub-divisional objectives. With the increase in both the size and the responsibilities carried by civilian staff, it is essential that they also are integrated into the team. Civilian staff have both service-provider roles and support roles, and the person who seeks assistance from the police expects excellent service irrespective of the status of the member of the police force. Although small team and sub-divisional identity are essential, the sub-divisional commander should not be parochial and fail to ensure that the sub-division is promoted positively as part of the larger force team.

Initially the team is used as a means of promoting the commitment and motivation of officers towards the goals of the force and standards of service. Then the team concept can be used to show individuals the importance of their contribution to the work done by others. The uniformed officer who responds to the scene of a crime should be aware that the officer who will continue the investigation relies on the responding officer's skill and work in his attempts to

detect the offender. This concept of internal quality is equally important in the context of such routine matters as paperwork and files.
The file submitted to the clerk in the administration support unit
should be of a sufficiently high standard to enable him or her to
complete the work without correcting errors or returning it to the
originating officer.

In some forces a rift can develop between operational officers and
their colleagues in headquarters departments. In principle, headquarters are established to help and support the work of operational
officers; however occasions can arise when the opposite appears to
be true. The co-ordination of effort must embrace headquarters
departments for them to reflect their supporting role. Methods must
be established for these departments to be sensitive to the work of
operational officers and to respond accordingly. During the fact-
finding phase, questions should be asked about the perceptions of
the support provided by headquarters departments. This process will
identify the positive and negative attitudes which are promoting and
inhibiting the sense of integration in the team.

Rewards system   An important goal of management strategy is to
encourage the behaviour of employees to be compatible with the
goals of the organisation and achieve excellent standards. Two simple
strategies can be used. First, appropriate behaviour can be rewarded
and second, undesirable behaviour can be punished. The difficulties
associated with direct supervision of officers on the streets make the
simple application of these two strategies something of a problem.
The most appropriate means of control is to develop a culture in
which the staff delivering services *want* to comply and conform to
the instructions and policies of the force and deliver a professional
service to the community. Therefore the police should use a means
of managerial control which exemplifies a positive attitude towards
the behaviour of staff. A control system compatible with the professional standards of the force will encourage compliance by high
professional standards of leadership.

This philosophy of management control which emphasises the positive or rewarding aspects of work should be extended to include a
learning approach to control. The police Discipline Code has the
problem of making individuals culpable for mistakes and therefore
the shortcomings or failings of the force as an organisation may be
overlooked. In the long term, more will be achieved if staff, and
the force in general, are able to learn from the errors of the past.
Thus a goal of the rewards system should be to create a culture of

self-improvement. Before staff can learn by their experience they must receive comments about their work from their supervisors. Opportunities must exist for staff to have this feedback as soon as possible after events. Giving feedback and counselling are skills which must be learned if they are to achieve the maximum benefits. It is very easy for the recipient of feedback to feel threatened by potential criticism and to take a defensive stance. If this does occur the opportunities for learning and self-development are substantially reduced. Therefore feedback mechanisms must be sensitive to the feelings of individuals.

Some research in a police force in the United States showed how the rewards system was in contradiction to the policy of the force.[8] The policy stated that the force was committed to community involvement priorities and encouraged officers in the community relations aspects of their work. However, when the records of transfer of officers on request, commendation for good work and promotions were examined, it was found that it was law enforcement work which was rewarded. Furthermore, when police officers were observed in their work, it was law enforcement activities they saw as priorities. The lesson is simple: rewards given to police officers should be compatible with the mission. The challenge is to develop definitions of services which meet community expectations, monitor their delivery and reward staff for excellent results.

Conflict and competition   Competition and friendly rivalry between groups of officers can be a source of motivation and encourage officers to achieve better results. Unfortunately the dividing line between the positive aspects of competition and the negative consequences of conflict is not always recognised. Where competition is based on unequal opportunities, a danger exists for damage to the team spirit of the working group. Uniformed officers achieve satisfaction from detecting crime, but if they believe they are given only those crimes with little chance of detection because crimes with more chance of resolution are kept by the CID (Criminal Investigation Department), competition turns to conflict. The uniformed officers feel they are being denied opportunities for success. Information received by area constables can be important in the detection of crime by other officers, but the chances of information being passed to other officers is reduced when area constables believe they will receive no recognition for their contribution to the detection of a crime. Thus conflict of individual interests can lead to a reduction in the overall achievements of the force. For competition to be positive, all staff have to believe there is an equal distribution of resources and opportunities to succeed.

Competition can motivate the achievements of officers when it is managed within a context which is constructive. If competition is used to show the weaknesses or inadequacies of individuals or groups, or if being better than another group becomes the only goal to be achieved, then competition will become destructive and change to conflict. People will become anxious and defensive. They will not co-operate with each other in case the other group takes advantage of the situation and claims the achievement on their own behalf. Competition, when it is constructive, can lead to innovation and promotes the use of imaginative solutions to policing problems. Conflict, however, can suppress innovation because individuals or groups fearing failure will continue to use existing methods.

Staff Surveys : Reviewing the Evidence

The audit of the culture and management style is a fact-finding exercise to provide information to assist in the planning and decision-making process which will precede the development of strategies to enable the force to meet community expectations. In the review of the information which is collected key questions should be asked to provide a framework of interpretation.

Communication
1 Do managers feel they have sufficient information to monitor performance and to make informed decisions?
2 Do problem-solving ideas regularly come from staff, or do they simply identify problems without providing solutions?
3 Do staff feel that they have a responsibility for, and are able to contribute to, the process of developing the force?

Decision making
1 Are decisions made by the staff closest to the problems?
2 Do staff feel authority levels are clearly defined and understood?
3 Do staff seek responsibilities or avoid them?
4 Do managers develop and grow to take on additional responsibilities?

Allocation of work
1 Is work allocated on the basis of the optimum use of staff?
2 Are there systems established to review work regularly and determine its current contribution to meeting community expectations?

3   Are workloads and resource allocations regularly reviewed and adjusted?

Team work
1   Are the efforts of individuals integrated to gain the optimum results from their work?
2   Do staff share a sense of common mission and goals?
3   Is there a sense of delivering internal quality to colleagues?
4   Is there an understanding of the contribution made by headquarters departments to the overall mission?

Rewards systems
1   Is there a sense of commitment to excellent services?
2   If service standards are not achieved, do staff believe the cause to be systems or individuals?
3   Are staff encouraged to develop and expand their responsibilities?
4   Do staff feel the rewards systems are related to meeting community expectations?

Conflict and competition
1   Is competition seen as encouraging commitment and motivation?

It is unlikely that any force will be suffering from all the problems associated with the culture and style of the force which have been described. Furthermore it would be dangerous to make the assumption that the problems do exist within the force or the sub-division. The manager's task is to review his own situation, determine the culture and style, and establish its impact on promoting or inhibiting delivery of excellent services.

Notes

1   A. J. P. Butler, *A Study of the Occupational Perceptions of Police Officers*, Doctoral Thesis, Faculty of Law, University of Birmingham (1979).
2   A. J. P. Butler and K. Tharme, *The Chelmsley Wood Policing Experiment*, Birmingham: West Midlands Police (1983).
3   A. J. P. Butler and K. Tharme, *A Survey of the Tasks of Permanent Beat Officers and the Opinions of their Supervisors*, Birmingham: West Midlands Police (1983).
4   E. Reuss-Ianni and F. A. J. Ianni, Street Cops and Management Cops: The Two Cultures of Policing', in M. Punch (ed.), *Control in the Police Organisation*, Cambridge, Mass.: The MIT Press.

5 A. J. P. Butler, *Occupational Perceptions*.
6 *Effective Policing – Performance Review in Police Forces*, The Audit Commission Police Paper Number 8, London (1990).
7 M. J. Hirst, 'The Development of Professional Excellence', *Policing*, **5**, 170–80 (1989).
8 S. W. Nadel, 'Measurement Systems and Organisational Goals in a Large Metropolitan Police Department', *Police Studies*, Figure 1, (3), 3–45 (1978).

6 Fact Finding: Identifying Community Expectations

In the past ten years there has been a considerable interest in questions concerned with police effectiveness and the efforts to make police services more efficient. In this debate there has on occasions been the mistaken belief that the pursuit of greater effectiveness and efficiency somehow compromises the achievement of 'quality'.

This chapter is concerned with pursuing this important consideration in the context of establishing from the public what they want the police to do and how it should be done. The values of our society would suggest that a police force should not strive for absolute effectiveness and efficiency without considering the wishes of the community. To achieve these two goals but to lose the support and confidence of society would be to pay too high a price. Community involvement and influence on policing policy are fundamental prerequisites of the style of policing which has developed in Britain. The task of the manager is to establish the means by which the diverse and sometimes contradictory demands of groups in society can be identified and assessed. Police forces must have formal mechanisms which include the consideration of these demands in their process of defining strategic policy.

The key points of this chapter are:

1 To understand how the community's needs and wishes should be included in the process of policy formation.
2 To recognise the limitations of traditional methods of assessing community needs.
3 To understand the management requirements for objective methods of assessing community needs.
4 To recognise the means by which the quality of police services can be measured.
5 To understand the uses of public surveys as an aid to police management.

6   To have a knowledge of the basic requirements of public survey techniques.
7   To understand how survey techniques can be adapted to suit particular information requirements.

The Nature of Community Expectations

There are two perspectives from which to approach the determination of community expectations. The first is to take a global view of the whole community, all the people living on a sub-division, or in a small town or housing estate. The second is to identify individual customers of services – the victim of a crime, the person asking for directions in the street, the witness to a road accident. The distinction may not be as real as the definitions might suggest, because the reaction of a witness may be determined by the overall attitudes to the police he has developed as a member of a particular community. However for practical purposes the distinction has to be made to enable a system to be developed to determine community expectations.

Community-wide Expectations

The need for more formal consultation methods with all sections of society was recognised by Lord Scarman, who recommended the nation-wide introduction of local consultation committees. The recommendation subsequently became part of the Police and Criminal Evidence Act 1984. There are many reasons for forming local consultation committees, but it is their role in assisting with the identification of community expectations which will be discussed.

The success of these arrangements will depend upon a number of factors, not least the quality of police/public relations and the ability to achieve a consensus on solutions to local policing problems. It is clear that these committees do represent another challenge to the skill and professionalism of police management. A number of management questions are raised by the formation of the committees:

1   Can the information which is obtained through the consultation process be seen as reliable and valid for the purposes of making policy?
2   Can this information be used as a basis upon which improvements in the quality of police services can be measured?

3   What influence should the committees be able to exert on the policy of the police?
4   The Home Office Circular says the arrangements should be 'effective in practice'. How will this be ensured? What characteristics will identify an effective consultative arrangement when compared with an ineffective arrangement?
5   Do the committees represent the views of the people they purport to represent?

These questions concern three main themes – the matter of the reliability and validity of the issues raised by the consultative committees, the utility of these data as performance measures, and the quality of the internal police policy-making process. A case study will serve to illustrate the first two points.

Case Study

A housing estate had been identified by a sub-divisional superintendent as having serious crime problems and as a response he formed a group of eight constables, supervised by a sergeant, to give added police cover to the area. After the first year of its operation a progress report claimed some success in dealing with the problems. The report recommended extending the policing method by forming a similar group of police officers to provide special policing cover for another area of the sub-division, known as Foleshill. This recommendation was supported by the views of local community leaders and politicians, from whom the sub-division enjoyed considerable support and co-operation. The Foleshill area was said by the community leaders to have a serious crime problem; there was a lack of confidence in the police, police visibility was said to be low and there was said to be racial tension. It was claimed that these problems were more serious there than in other areas of the city. The enthusiasm of the local council could be measured by their proposal to provide several thousand pounds to assist with the provision of a police section station to accommodate the police officers posted to the proposed team.

It is worth examining the evidence available to the senior officers when deciding on the most appropriate course of action. In common with many policing initiatives at the time, the review of the performance of the initial policing project on the housing estate was based exclusively on subjective perceptions. When apparently objective measures were included, such as crime and vandalism figures, these relied entirely on the assumption that either all such incidents were reported to the police or that the proportions being reported before and during the life of the project remained unchanged. Neither assumption could be supported on the research evidence. Thus it was impossible to measure the improvements achieved in crime control by this additional police manpower. Any claims to having improved the public's awareness of the increased presence of police officers, or to having reduced their fear of crime or improved their satisfaction with the police, could not hope to be sustained in the total absence of objective evidence. Thus a replication of the policing project in a different community could not be justified simply by the results achieved on the housing estate.

If previous experience did not provide information on which to make the managerial decision, how could the arguments made by the local community leaders and politicians be viewed? Did they provide a sound basis on which to proceed to deploy several police officers at considerable cost to the force? The questions could not be answered. The case for change was being made on personal opinions and beliefs. The Chief Constable decided that, before the proposals were implemented, some questions should be answered with objective evidence:

1   What was the true nature of the policing problems?
2   How did these problems manifest themselves and what were the measures of police effectiveness?
3   What policy options did the analysis suggest?
4   If changes were to be made to the policing methods, what specific objectives were to be pursued?
5   After the changes had been implemented what measures could be used for evaluating the results?

We can again see the cyclical nature of this problem-solving exercise. The performance measures identified at 2 are readily available to be measured in the evaluation stage 5.

The views expressed by the local leaders provided the starting-point for the objective investigation. Two officers examined the views expressed by the community leaders and prepared a means of testing these issues with the residents. Of the four issues identified, only one, the crime problem, had a data source within the force. However the problem of unreported crime made the use of police statistics unreliable. If it was true there was a lack of confidence in the police, then a large amount of crime might not be reported. Improved confidence in the police might apparently generate more crime by increasing the proportion of crime being reported to the police.

To obtain the necessary information a direct survey of the residents of Foleshill was suggested to measure their experience of, and their attitudes to, crime and the police. A similar survey was suggested for the remaining area of the city to make some comparisons between the two groups of people. A questionnaire was developed and a random sample of a thousand residents of Foleshill was approached by interviewers who recorded their responses on the questionnaire. A similar survey was made of a random sample of 300 people from elsewhere in the city. The survey and the data were collected and analysed by the internal resources of the force.

The questionnaire sought to obtain information from the residents to provide an assessment of the present effectiveness of the policing of Foleshill compared with the rest of the city. The survey was also designed to provide data which could be used as a means of evaluating any improvements that had been achieved in the event of changes being made to the policing methods. Data on the following topics were obtained from the survey:

1 The frequency of the occurrence of a range of crimes and the proportions which were reported to the police.
2 The frequency of sightings by the residents of the police and contact between them and the police.
3 General attitudes towards the police and satisfaction with various aspects of the service which they provided.
4 Public perceptions of the seriousness of a range of crimes and social problems which were mainly concerned with issues which influenced the residents' perceptions of public tranquillity in their neighbourhoods.

The data obtained from the survey in Foleshill questioned the conclusions drawn by the community leaders. When these data were compared with the responses obtained from the citizens living elsewhere in the city, there were few differences in the experiences and attitudes.

When the results of this survey were presented to police management and conveyed to the community leaders, it was obvious to all concerned that the problems apparently afflicting this community were no more severe than those afflicting other communities throughout the city. Furthermore, in some respects, the police enjoyed more confidence in Foleshill than elsewhere. While these results should not be taken as showing that there were no problems in the community, it is management's responsibility to ensure that resources are used equitably throughout the force on the basis of the priorities identified through community needs. Thus the proposal to establish a group of police officers with an exclusive responsibility for this area, based in a specially built section station, was abandoned in favour of a less radical proposal.

Policy Implications to be Drawn from the Case Study

The local politicians' and community leaders' views of the policing problems of Foleshill were not supported by the opinions of the residents. Therefore it would have been unwise to act solely upon information obtained through consultation with the local representatives, because it was not an accurate representation of the policing problems. Furthermore the opinions of community leaders could not have been used as a reliable and valid means of measuring subsequent police performance because the police, by changing their methods, would have been trying to meet community expectations and solve problems which did not exist.

The case study illustrates the importance of making a careful analysis of the existing situation before making plans to change. Without having accurate information about the community's expectations of police services it is impossible to meet them with any certainty. The consultation system has an important part to play in police/community relations and the process of determining community expectations, but it has some significant limitations which cannot be ignored. The process has to be a combination of subjective views and objective information.

The Service Audit

Determining Customer Expectations

The difficulty with determining the expectations of the 'wider community' is related to the identification of the people who comprise 'the community'. This difficulty does not arise when the expectation of customers of specific police services are being considered. It will be helpful to refer to this aspect of determining public expectations as the 'service audit'.

Implicit in the need to conduct a service audit is the recognition that the force cannot state in precise terms the standards of service the public will consistently receive from the force. The service audit responds to the three primary questions discussed in Chapter 2:

- What does the community expect the police to achieve for it?
- To what extent is the police force satisfying those expectations?
- If there are no reliable measures of community expectations and the extent to which the force is satisfying them, how can the force be sure of maintaining public confidence?

There are two principal objectives in the service audit: to obtain information from the customer and to identify what services are currently provided. The role of the service audit is to compare these two sets of information. Based on these two objectives the terms of reference of the service audit can be written as follows:

1 To identify those activities and tasks which can be categorised as part of one of the core services; for example, the 'responding to calls for assistance and advice' service.
2 To seek information from the consumers of those services about their expectations and to define service standards which would meet these expectations.
3 To measure existing service delivery against public expectations and identify over- and underachievement.
4 To document information which will identify inadequacies in monitoring service delivery standards, changes in the organisation of work, new services to be designed and delivered, changes in resource deployments and any other developments to bring service standards into line with community expectations.

The final step in the terms of reference goes beyond identifying the current position and the desired position, but it is important for the forums which will be considering the results of the service audit to have some understanding of the implications of the decision to make a commitment to achieving the service standards. Standards have to be set in the real world, with all the constraints that apply. There is little point setting targets which are not achievable; expectation may have to be modified, a process which will be described in Chapter 8.

The Steps in the Service Audit

The co-ordinator who has been appointed at chief officer level will identify individuals to form a project team to examine each core service using the terms of reference defined above. The project team will be chosen so as to enable a broad cross-section of expertise to be available. The project team will be briefed by the co-ordinator to ensure that the purpose, timescales and documentation formats are clearly understood. The briefing should include ground rules about data collection methods, access to expert advice and technical assistance in analysis and so forth.

Regular progress meetings should be held with the project team as a forum in which to discuss common problems, exchange information on developments and provide an opportunity for any redirection to occur. The project team will follow a predetermined pattern of steps to achieve their objectives:

1   Collate and categorise all the tasks and activities which appear to contribute to the delivery of the core service. There may be some need for the co-ordinator to make decisions as to the inclusion or exclusion of particular tasks.
2   Group these tasks around points of delivery. For example, in responding to calls for assistance or advice, several parts of the police force are involved, from the telephone switchboard, to the control room, to the officer visiting the scene of an incident.
3   Design a method of obtaining information from the customer of the service which will describe their expectations in ways which will enable standards of service to be defined. This process might take the form of visiting a category of customers, for example victims of house burglaries, to document what service they received and what they would have expected to receive. It might also involve the use of a questionnaire aimed at recent callers on police services. The trap to avoid is simply asking people if they are 'satisfied or dissatisfied' with the police. The answer to this question is not capable of being interpreted in a form which would allow any standards to be set because there is no way of knowing *why* they were satisfied or dissatisfied. If the reason for the response is unknown, how can service strategies be devised?
4   Using the results of step 2, the grouping of the tasks around the delivery points, identify those existing measures of service delivery. It is possible that there will be few, if any. Where few exist, a decision will have to be taken on what steps will be needed

immediately to fill this information gap. It may be necessary to suspend the progress of the group to enable service standard measures to be designed and used to collect sufficient data on which to judge the 'here and now'. When sufficient information is available, public expectations can be assessed against current standards of delivery.

5   Using the results of the analysis of step 4, produce charts to compare public expectation with current standards for each point in the service delivery process. These charts will identify over- and underachieving.

6   The final step is the production of the document which covers (1) public expectations; (2) current levels of service delivery achieved by individual parts of the force; (3) a profile of standards of service delivery for this core function; (4) proposals to reduce levels of service where necessary without damaging public expectations; (5) proposals to increase levels of service to meet public expectations, describing resource and other implications; (6) a method of monitoring service delivery standards; (7) a method of feedback to relevant managers of service delivery performance; and (8) an outline description of all issues which need to be considered in the context of strategic policy to develop longer-term improvements to service delivery.

When this document has been produced there will be a need to consider it in the context of current organisational practice, procedures and structure. It will also be important to consider the staff aspects of the issues raised.

Measuring Public Expectations

The value of obtaining objective information about community expectations cannot be overstated. Police work is one of those professions on which everyone is an expert, and the solution to problems is always looking backwards to some mythical golden age. Police managers who have the responsibility for protecting and serving the public cannot indulge themselves in the same nostalgia. They cannot afford the luxury of guessing about the expectations or the public or jumping to ill-conceived conclusions about how these expectations could be satisfied. Consequently surveys of the public are an essential management tool, both in the planning and determination of police tactics, and in the measurement of results. It is essential that the information they provide should be reliable and valid. Therefore such surveys should not be undertaken without a clear understanding of the problems and pitfalls. A full description of the techniques and practical considerations of public surveys is outside the purpose of this book. Attention will be restricted to the consideration of the management aspects of surveys, such as the reasons for conducting a survey, the administration and logistics and the advantages of various survey methods.

Why Conduct a Survey?

The simple answer to this question is 'to determine public expectations'. Surveys are an important part of the fact-finding process. The results of the survey will influence future policy and service standards, so it must be planned and conducted in a disciplined and structured manner.

Before any decisions are made concerning the need to commission a public attitude survey, the specific information requirements of the policing problem should be carefully defined. The manager should ask himself why he needs the information and what purpose it will serve when he has obtained it. Consider the simple example of a sub-divisional superintendent who is being asked by his local consultative committee to use more officers to patrol on foot. A simple response to this demand would be to reduce the number of mobile patrols and deploy the officers on foot. A more thoughtful response would be to consider the advantages to be gained from such a change. Local community representatives might claim advantages, with such comments as, 'It will reduce public fear of crime', 'It will improve public satisfaction with the police', or 'It will reduce crime through the deterrent effect of more visible police', but despite these statements negative consequences are also possible. Reducing the mobility of the police could produce complaints about delays in responding to calls from the public and reductions in detection rates for crime because of slower responses to crimes in progress. The proposal to increase the number of foot patrol officers also identifies the range of information which may be required to evaluate the results of the change.

Surveys are an essential part of the process of determining how the public feel about current services and what deficiency they perceive in them. The earlier part of this chapter described the process of auditing core services and referred to the involvement of customers. Although these surveys are likely to be on a smaller scale, they must be based on the same structured and disciplined principles which apply to all public surveys.

The third purpose which can be served by survey data is to provide the means of evaluating the consequences of changes to policing methods or service delivery standards. 'Before and after' surveys are one of the most powerful means of determining the extent to which changes in police services are meeting community expectations; they can be used to measure the change at global levels, for example in the increase in police visibility, or at a more specific level, as through changes to services to burglary victims.

Are there Existing Sources of Data?

Surveys do not take place in isolation. They are not an end in themselves but part of a fact-finding process within the system of problem identification. Consequently the results will form only one part of the information which will be considered in the development process. Therefore, as part of the planning for a survey, existing sources of information must be identified. It is also possible that an existing source of information may question the need for a survey. For example, most control rooms have tape-recording systems for all the calls received from the public. An analysis of the information collected during these calls could reduce the scope of a public survey of callers, or even eliminate the need for it.

In cases where a public survey is required, additional data sources must be identified to create the context in which the results of the survey can be set. The richer this context, the more valuable are the individual pieces of information. In many cases the value of the whole can be greater than the sum of the parts.

What are the Administrative Requirements for a Public Survey?

When the need for a direct survey of the public has been established, practical considerations must be addressed. The force must have someone who understands the technical requirements of conducting surveys, or they must have direct access to a person who is prepared to give the necessary support to the force throughout the process. There is no point receiving technical assistance in preparing the survey, if that help is not continued to assist in the interpretation of data. One course would be to hand the technical aspects to a commercial organisation or an academic institution. This has some advantages but may be expensive; it also has a number of other disadvantages. For example, if the project is referred to external experts, the force will need to retain careful control of the management of the project to ensure that the data are suitable for their purpose.

The survey will require a project leader or co-ordinator and an assistant or office manager. The administration of a survey involves the technical knowledge which is required at various times throughout the project and the continuing day-to-day administration. These tasks should be split between two people. Depending on the survey method chosen, there will be a need for people to distribute, collate and analyse the responses. Unless the survey is very rudimentary and on a small scale, some computer facilities will be required to analyse the questionnaires. The availability of these resources, manpower and technical aids will determine the timescale for the completion of the survey.

What Methods Should be Used?

The choice of survey method should be related to the information requirements. The more complex the information required then the more sophisticated the method of collection. To obtain detailed information about what services were given to the victim of a burglary and to extend the information to identify unfulfilled expectations, a face-to-face interview is the only viable option. However, to seek some basic information about the service provided by a control room to a motorist reporting mechanical failures on a motorway, a well-designed postal questionnaire will suffice.

The postal survey technique has the advantages of a simpler administration and lower cost, but there are a number of disadvantages. It requires a very careful construction of the questionnaire to make sure that it can be understood by the people who are asked to complete it, because there is no opportunity to clarify ambiguous questions, as with a trained interviewer. Another substantial disadvantage is the sometimes high proportion of people who fail to respond to the survey. The person selected by the sampling procedure can never be guaranteed to be the person who actually completes the questionnaire, which can lead to distortions in the sample.

The alternative method is to use a questionnaire as a structured interview format which is used by interviewers who interview the person selected by a random sampling procedure. The questionnaire is then completed by the interviewer on the basis of responses given by the subject. Using this method there is less opportunity for the sample to be contaminated because it is the selected person who responds to the questionnaire. The questions can be relatively more sophisticated and complex as the interviewer can guide the subject through the procedure by careful questioning and probing. The interviewer is also available to clarify any ambiguities or misunderstandings which may arise from time to time. Finally, when a person declines to take part in the survey, it is possible with the use of an interviewer to determine the reasons for the refusal. It can never be assumed that the reason people do not take part in surveys concerning the police is that they do not like the police.

There is no right or wrong answer to the question, 'Which method is best?' The decision has to be made after a careful consideration of the needs of the fact-finding exercise.

How will the Information be Collected?

If there is one area to be singled out as having a critical requirement for professional advice and expertise, it is the design of questionnaires. If the data have been obtained using inadequately designed questions, the whole process is a wasted effort. The basic rules for questionnaire design follow a simple pattern. The subject areas for questions can be identified through the process of defining the objectives of a specific police service or range of services and the criteria on which service standards are measured. The researcher has to translate those objectives and service standards into suitably phrased questions which will reliably and validly produce data related to the objectives. No questionnaire should be used without undertaking an appropriate pilot study. The value of pilot studies cannot be overemphasised, because this is the only way in which a questionnaire design can be tested before it is used in the main study. As much care should be taken with the pilot study as with the main study; for example, it is not adequate to invite colleagues in the office to complete a questionnaire which is going to be used to measure schoolchildren's attitudes towards police officers. Similarly, if a survey is to be used to sample the opinions of all sections of the community, it will be pointless conducting a pilot study only in a middle-class residential area.

In addition to questions related to a direct measurement of the objectives of the study, the researcher must consider the influence on the subjects' responses of social and demographic variables, such as the age and sex of the respondent and the type of housing in which he or she lives. These demographic variables are important for subsequent analysis because people's opinions may vary according to the area in which they live, and there may also be differences between men and women or between young and old, or between people who live in their own house and those who live in rented accommodation. A further purpose of these data is to test the sampling method used.

A final consideration in the design of a questionnaire is to consider the means by which the data will be analysed. In most circumstances a computer will be used to perform this task and therefore it is essential at the design stage to ensure that the questionnaire is also suitable as a computer input document. It may be that the survey is to be conducted within the force, but that the data input and analysis are to be performed by some other agency. If this is the case, liaison must be established at an early stage between the project director and the agency who will undertake the data input and analysis. If this does not occur the agency may refuse to input the data directly from the questionnaire and require the force to transfer thousands of items from questionnaires onto some approved input document.

There are a number of computer programs available for analysing data. One of the more widely used programs should be chosen for this purpose, such as the Statistical Package for the Social Sciences.[1] Before choosing the computer program consideration must be given to the size of database which the program is capable of handling and the statistical routines which the program can perform to ensure not only that frequency counts and averages are produced, but that the data are also capable of being examined for underlying trends and predictive relationships.

Who will Provide the Information?

The purpose of a public survey is to establish data which are a true reflection of a wider population's attitudes or opinions. The term population is used to describe the total number of people who comprise the group who are under examination. Thus, if information is required from people who have been the victim of a burglary in the past year, the total population is the total number of people who have reported a burglary in the last 12 months. The most accurate means by which that population's opinions and attitudes could be measured would be to interview each person and give them the opportunity of responding to the questionnaire. Even with a population as small as 10 000, it would not be practicable to obtain questionnaire responses from every single person, so the survey has to sample the population. A sample is the number of people taken from the total population in such a way that the attitudes and opinions of the sample reliably reflect the opinions and attitudes which would have been expressed if all the people within the population had been questioned. Therefore, when considering sampling, there are three overriding criteria which must be determined: identification of the target population; establishing the means of selection; and determining the size of the sample which will be required to ensure their opinions and attitudes reliably reflect those of the total population.

To a certain extent the size of the sample is a compromise between the need for reliable and valid data and the practical considerations of time and cost. The extent of sampling error which can be tolerated within the survey can be obtained from standard texts on the subject.[2] There are two other considerations when determining the sample; first, there will be a number of people who will decline the invitation to take part and, second, the method of selecting the people in the sample must be unbiased.

How will the Project be Managed?

Irrespective of the survey method or the size of the sample, the process should be carefully planned and the steps in the project documented to include clear guidelines for the staff taking part. The project plan must contain the following information:

1 the survey objectives;
2 the key information requirements;
3 the relationship of the survey information to other additional information;
4 the type of survey method to be used;
5 the questionnaire development process, including pilot studies;
6 determining the sample size and the selection method;
7 instructions for undertaking the data collection, with training schedules where these are required for interviewers, for example;
8 quality assurance methods for the data collection;
9 procedures for data collation, processing and analysis; and
10 framework for the presentation of the results.

How will the Information be Handled?

The precise nature of the analysis to be performed on data will depend entirely upon the purpose of the survey and the nature of the data. A researcher should avoid at all costs the temptation to dredge through data producing masses of statistics in the hope of finding some interesting or significant results. At the data analysis stage the project director should return to the original objectives of the survey and translate those objectives into useful working hypotheses. An objective of a policing method may be a reduction in the fear of crime by increasing the number of uniformed foot patrol officers and thereby increasing public awareness of a police presence. Therefore an appropriate hypothesis to be explored in that case would be as follows: 'There is a relationship between the citizen's awareness of the uniformed police presence in the neighbourhood and their fear of crime.' When the hypothesis has been established, it is a simple task to identify from the questionnaire those questions relating to police visibility and citizens' fear of crime. The computer can then be used to examine the relationship between the two factors.

Before seizing upon results as demonstrating support for a hypothesis, the significance of the relationship must be considered. This interpretation involves some knowledge of statistical techniques and, in particular, levels of statistical significance. If the researcher does not have this knowledge then expert advice should be sought.

Where the information requirements are less complex, the same rigour should be applied to the information, as when, for example, the questionnaires are returned through the post by people who requested help from the police when they were stranded on the motorway. The responses have to be analysed in the context of the reasons for which the information was collected. Where only a small proportion respond, the conclusions drawn from the answers have to be set in that context.

Concluding Comments

The process of obtaining information which describes community needs and expectations is a critical part of future policing strategy. If the process is flawed then the information will not provide the reliable and valid foundation on which the force can develop its responses. There are evident dangers in attempting to cross a desert with a faulty compass. The analogy holds if unreliable information is used to design new service delivery systems. If in doubt seek expert advice, but do not take a chance on the information being correct: the results may create more problems than currently exist.

Notes

1 N. H. Nie, C. Hadlaihull, J. G. Jenkins, K. Steinbrenner and D. H. Bent, *Statistical Package for the Social Sciences*, New York: McGraw-Hill Inc. (1975).
2 G. Hoinville, R. Jowell, *et al.*, *Survey Research Practice*, London: Heinemann Educational Books Ltd (1977).

7 Fact Finding: Organising Systems and Staff

The second stage of the management cycle is concerned with the organising of resources, which in a manpower-intensive organisation such as the police makes the use of staff a very important concern. Before a manager can consider changes in the organisation of his staff he must establish the existing use and effectiveness of those resources. Thus two general issues will be discussed in this chapter: the means of reviewing the present use and effectiveness of staff, and methods of reorganising those resources to achieve improvements in performance leading towards achieving the mission. Although the techniques described in this chapter are part of the fact-finding process, they are also concerned with using information gathered in the staff and service audits to build a more effective organisation of staff.

The key points of this chapter are:

1 To understand why the planning stage of the management cycle requires an examination of the way in which the organisation of staff influences service delivery standards.
2 To be able to define the purpose of organisational structures.
3 To understand the need to examine the organisational structure within the framework of the methods of supervision and management, the co-ordination of resources, the procedures and systems in use, the clarity of the responsibilities and authority of individuals, and the knowledge and skills of individuals.
4 To be able to analyse an organisational structure, identify its component sub-systems and the relationships between the sub-systems.
5 To recognise the need to relate the organisational structure to the mission.
6 To understand how police systems and procedures influence service delivery standards.

7   To understand the contribution organisation and methods techniques can make to the analysis and improvements of systems and procedures.

8   To understand the need to identify the constituent tasks of police work.

9   To recognise the contributions made by the knowledge, skills and attitudes of staff to the performance of their tasks.

10   To understand the compilation, use and value of job descriptions for individual postholders and managers.

11   To understand methods which can be used to determine the appropriate level of human resources and their organisation to respond to a given workload.

12   To understand how these techniques can be applied to solve service delivery problems.

Definition and Purpose of an Organisational Structure

The purpose of the structure is to organise staff, police and civilians, to optimise their performance in pursuit of the mission of the force. It is the means by which the staff are arranged to the greatest advantage, judged against their ability to achieve the goals. Therefore the appropriateness of the organisational structure of a force should be judged on the results it produces and no other criteria.

The effectiveness of the organisational structure can only be evaluated by reference to the mission and the goals of the police force. A manager must assess the contribution the staff under his command are making to the achievement of the goals. The organisation of these resources and the procedures they follow will have a significant effect on the results produced. To bring a framework to the analysis of the organisational structure seven areas can be identified and used by the manager to examine his own situation:

1   The mission – unless there is a clear understanding of the mission and the means by which results will be measured, the organisation will lack a sense of direction and a reference point from which to relate its work.

2   A knowledge of community expectations – the structure of police organisations should be directly related to the services being delivered in response to community expectations.

3   Quality assurance – the methods and measures of day-to-day

monitoring and longer-term evaluation of the achievement of service standards.

4 Co-ordination of resources – the methods of ensuring that all officers are aware of, and are pursuing, common objectives and delivering services to the required standards.

5 Procedures and systems – these must be compatible with the objectives of the organisation and not take more time or resources than is absolutely necessary to ensure quality assurance.

6 Clarity of responsibilities and authority – staff should be aware of the extent of their decision-making discretion and their responsibilities for achieving the mission and goals.

7 Individual knowledge and skills – matched to the tasks and standards of service which individuals are called upon to perform and achieve.

The seven points summarised above are the key elements essential to the effective organisational structure. They should be reviewed regularly by managers to make sure they are still consistent with the mission and goals. Changes, inside and outside the force, may require modifications to the organisational structure to retain standards of service delivery.

Organisational Audit

Sub-divisional Organisation: a Case Study

The sub-division as the basic operational unit serves as a good example to illustrate the issues which have to be addressed when looking at the influence of the organisational structure on the ability of the force to meet community expectations. The structure of a typical sub-division is shown in Figure 7.1. There are three sub-systems: the uniformed patrol officers who provide the 24-hour police function, some investigative tasks, reassurance patrols and community contact; the Criminal Investigation Department (CID) who are responsible for the investigation of more serious crimes; and the support and specialist sub-system which is comprised of a plain-clothes squad, local intelligence officer and clerical and administrative support. An organisational diagram is a very useful means of identifying the component parts of an organisation, the relationship between the parts and the numbers of staff who are available to the manager.

The purpose of the organisational structure is to make optimum

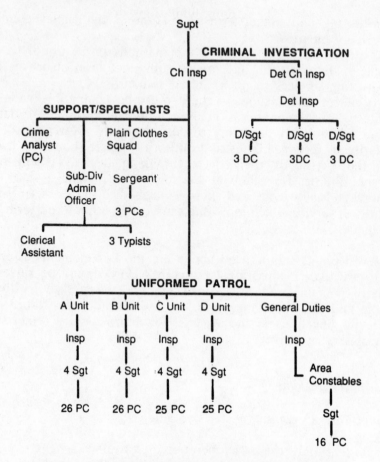

Figure 7.1 Sub-divisional organisational diagram

use of available resources. Therefore in the planning stage of the management cycle the organisational structure has to be examined in the context of the extent to which it facilitates the satisfaction of community expectations, and the need for changes to improve performance. Historically sub-divisional structures have developed without being consistently linked to the quality of services required by the public. The purpose of the organisational audit is (1) to determine the current standards of service being delivered; (2) to compare current standards of service with the expectation of the community; and (3) to structure the resources to achieve the standards expected by the community.

At the start of this process there has to be an acceptance of the ideal, namely the congruence of community expectations with the standards of service delivered. In reality there may be some compromise between the two because of the limits placed on resources. The purpose of the case study is to raise some questions which will assist the process of analysis, leading to the possible restructuring of the sub-divisional resources. The seven points identified above will be used as a framework for the analysis.

The mission The analysis must start with a definition of the mission of the force which will be translated into goals. Although an understanding of the mission and goals and the consequent responsibilities of the sub-division are essential factors in the successful achievement of the mission, there has been well-documented evidence that the typical constable does not feel part of a corporate effort and is uncertain about the extent to which his work contributes to the overall mission. In the light of this evidence the sub-divisional commander has to ask himself some searching questions. How certain is he of the mission of the force? If he asked ten members of his sub-division to describe the mission, would he receive ten different answers? Can he measure the extent to which the work of his subdivision is achieving the mission?

When the sub-divisional commander cannot refer to some definitive statement of mission by the Chief Constable, he will have to rely on a reasonable interpretation of existing force policy statements. This may not be a significant disadvantage because some writers on the topic of organisational mission suggest starting with a theme which, over a period of time, through responding to the needs of the customer, will develop into a mission statement.[1] In the absence of a defined mission statement, a theme, such as 'meeting community expectations' is a good starting-point.

A knowledge of community expectations Assuming the mission is meeting community expectations, it is essential to know what they are. Techniques for collecting information about community expectations were described in Chapter 6 as the service audit. The information which was documented in the service audit will form an essential element in the process of creating staff structures and procedures to provide services to meet community expectations. Where the service audit has shown that current services are not meeting these expectations, structures and procedures must be considered as a possible contributory factor. The sub-divisional commander should be aware of the dangers of attempting to move too far too fast. He should perhaps consider which areas of service he is going to develop first to meet community expectations. When these are in place, he can develop others, moving towards synchronisation of expectations and delivery standards in a series of steps.

Quality assurance   Traditional styles of supervision and management have been concerned with meeting internally set standards: filling in the crime report correctly, emphasising the administration, rather than ensuring that the needs of the burglary victim have been met. If the paperwork was correct and there was no formal complaint, there was an implicit assumption in this style of supervision that the work was to the required standards and by implication must have satisfied the customer. If there were no defined standards of service which reflected the expectations of the community, it was hardly the fault of the sergeant or inspector if he continued to perform his role in this way.

Supervision and management are empty words in the absence of defined standards of service. The sub-divisional commander should ask himself what he means by these terms. What is he expecting his staff to supervise? What are the standards by which the sub-division will be judged? There will continue to be a need to maintain administrative standards but these will be linked directly to meeting customer needs; for example, if incorrect information is entered on a report, it may cause a problem for a victim of crime, or cause another member of staff to waste time making a correction.

Co-ordination of resources   A major problem for all managers is the task of co-ordinating the efforts of all their resources towards common objectives. Problems of co-ordination can be caused by a number of factors, from a simple neglect of the importance of communication within the organisation to shift patterns which reduce the opportunities for officers to meet and discuss policing problems and to devise common approaches to deal with them. A potentially serious aspect which inhibits the co-ordination of resources is the lack of a shared understanding of the mission and the ways in which community expectations are going to be met. Just as the sergeant or inspector may be vague about the standards of service he should expect from his staff, so the staff delivering the service may also ask questions about what is expected of them.

Co-ordination presupposes some common purpose and direction. The sub-divisional commander must ask himself, 'Can I be sure all the staff know our objectives, the way we are going to achieve them and the standards of service?' If the answer is 'No', there is some basic work to be undertaken to ensure that he can answer the questions and then communicate the key points to his staff.

Procedures and systems   The administrative procedures used on the sub-division will not be immediately apparent from the examination of the structure, but this is a useful place to start to look for the ways in which the various parts communicate with each other and are co-ordinated through the administration processes. Procedures and systems can have a significant impact on the performance of the sub-division. There are a number of useful questions the sub-divisional commander can ask about procedures and systems, but there has to be a framework of reference to direct them and make sense of the answers. Procedures and systems consume valuable time and other resources, irrespective of their contribution to the achievement of the mission. The frame of reference as a starting-point for the questioning should be the context of the core services. To what extent do the systems contribute to the satisfaction of community expectations? Do procedures have clearly-defined quality standards which can be monitored? How is supervision viewed?

Paradoxically, if the role of supervision is seen as a safety net to catch and remedy poor-quality work, it can work against the concept of 'doing it right first time'. How much time and energy is spent by supervision in this role of correcting other people's mistakes? The critical test of a procedure or system is to ask, 'What would happen and who would notice if it was abandoned?'

Clarity of responsibilities and authority   Although people are organised in a structure such as the one shown in Figure 7.1, it cannot be assumed that they have a clear understanding of exactly what is expected of them and the authority they have over other people or to make decisions. These are all matters which should be included in job descriptions, which may be available for some officers and civilians. Where job descriptions exist they should be reviewed to ensure that they are still relevant to the tasks being performed by the postholder. Where job descriptions do not exist serious consideration should be given to developing them. Individuals must know how their tasks fit into the total efforts of the organisation. They must have a point of reference for them to identify their responsibilities and the limits of their accountabilities. All work involves decision making, therefore individuals must know the limits of their authority to make decisions and those matters which must be referred to a higher authority. Where confusion exists over responsibilities the usual consequence is the passing of problems and decisions further up the hierarchy until someone is prepared to make the decision.

Individual knowledge and skills   Another assumption which a manager cannot make concerns the competency of his staff. A manager has the responsibility of ensuring that the knowledge and skills of his staff are appropriate for the tasks they are expected to fulfil.

Consider the role of the local intelligence officer. There are different levels of knowledge and skill required for this work, depending upon the job description. If the role is seen as recording and indexing reported crime and information from operational officers, the work is less demanding than a role which requires an integrated crime analysis service, where information is extracted and interpreted to indicate crime trends, patrol deployment strategies and avenues for investigation. When the role has been defined, it is the manager's responsibility to make sure that the postholder has the necessary skills and knowledge.

This consideration is true for all posts. Furthermore a manager should try to predict the future human resource needs of his sub-division and train people before they are given the responsibilities. Of course this may involve the force training department or other specialists who would be given notice of the training requirements to enable them to plan ahead. This process can provide the impetus for career development programmes in the force.

Response to the Organisational Audit

Following his questioning of the structure, the sub-divisional commander is likely to find a number of important points unanswered. Put simply, he will probably be uncertain as to the extent of his knowledge about the quality of the work his staff are producing and to what extent they are delivering services which meet community expectations. If he is being held accountable for the delivery of services then his first concern must be to establish and document the services being provided.

The difficulties presented by the need to match services to community expectation should not be underestimated, so it is important to adopt a practical and realistic approach to the task. Core services, such as receiving and handling telephone calls and the investigation of crime, should perhaps be considered first. The techniques can then be applied to more services as experience and expertise develop.

Step 1 Determine the Current Standards of Service Being Delivered

The starting-point is to document what is done now, by whom and where. This process involves identifying all the constituent tasks which are performed in the provision of the service. This may seem at first sight to be a fairly simple and irrelevant process, but until these tasks have been documented there is no objective basis on which to determine service standards. Furthermore it may surprise some people to learn how little or how much is being done, by such a wide range of people and at so many locations. Failures in service delivery are more likely to be caused by not properly defining what should be done, by not assigning tasks to people to make them accountable, by overcomplicating the systems, by making erroneous assumptions about what the public expects, and by failing to build in monitoring and feedback mechanisms than by a lack of commitment or motivation of staff. The majority of staff are committed to excellent service; it is the leadership and systems of the organisation which usually let them down.

The use of staff trained in the skills of organisation and methods work would be an advantage in this process, which should identify (1) the component parts of a system; (2) the relationship between parts of a system; (3) the people involved; and (4) the documents and equipment used. In addition to this documentation process it is also necessary to obtain some measurement of the work involved in performing individual tasks or groups of tasks. Work measurement can establish (1) the time each part of the process takes to complete; (2) the total time taken for the entire process; (3) a count of how often the process is performed in any given period; and (4) the total time needed to complete a specific workload.

When this first step has been completed information will have been collected about a specific service, such as completing the initial visit to the scene and recording a domestic burglary. This information will describe (1) all the tasks which should be completed; (2) the category of staff who are responsible for each task; (3) the average amount of time taken to complete each task; (4) the procedures and forms used; and (5) the links to the next stages in the process.

The process of documenting the constituent elements of a service will also produce a greater knowledge and understanding of the work being done by staff. It is a common experience for managers to realise during the course of this process the serious limitations of their knowledge. Comments such as 'I thought we stopped doing that years ago', and 'We could stop that tomorrow and it wouldn't make any difference to the service' are common. In the next stage the results of the internal service audit are compared with the expectations of the public.

Step 2   Compare Current Standards of Service with the Expectation of the Community

In the previous chapter, a method of recording community expectations was described. The information collected using this process can now be compared to the service delivery profile produced by step 1. Difficulties can arise through the volume of data involved in the process; the skill is to categorise tasks and expectations under various sub-categories and make comparisons between two columns of information – the right-hand column describing what the community expects and the left-hand column describing tasks currently undertaken. This method makes it possible for gaps to be seen where the public have an expectation which is not being met by an equivalent service task and, of equal importance, tasks will be seen to be performed where the public do not have an expectation of them.

Using the raw data comparison, decisions have to be made to define the standards for a particular service. The term 'standards' is used to describe what every person can expect from the police. The use of this term does not preclude a particular person receiving some additional services over and above those standards. However, unless some benchmark is set, staff will not know what is expected of them, the public will not be able to rely on the service standards being consistent across time and locations and managers will not be able to estimate the resources required to perform services or to adjust those resources if demands for the service increase or decrease.

Although there may be some elimination of current tasks and some requirements for additional tasks, the process of defining the standards has to take account of the resources available. There may be a need to negotiate a compromise between the 'ideal' service, as identified by community expectations, and the 'possible' which can be achieved within the resource limitations. This will be a test of the sub-divisional commander's skill in consulting the community and marketing the service to customers.

With the completion of step 2, a profile of the individual elements of a service will have been identified and related to community expectations. The next stage is to structure resources to achieve these standards.

Step 3 Structure the Resources to Achieve the Standards Expected by the Community

The third step in this process is concerned with identifying what needs to be done to deliver these service standards consistently. The comparison of service delivery with community expectations will have shown some examples of a significant failure of the current systems or structures to deliver the service. The case study later in the chapter illustrates this point. Improvements in the service could only be achieved by the introduction of a new system with additional staff. The development of new structures which will probably also include changes to the work of staff is a complex issue and has to be preceded by an analysis of all the tasks to identify the required skills, knowledge and attitudes to perform the role successfully. The value of task analysis increases as the complexity of the work increases. A useful way of understanding the role of task analysis is to imagine the process of instructing a completely inexperienced person to perform a task. The starting-point of the teaching process would be to provide the person with all the necessary knowledge.

In the case of a constable who was being instructed in the enforcement of road traffic law, he would have to have a detailed knowledge of legislation; he would require information concerning the procedures and forms to be used in the process of reporting a motorist; and he would require a knowledge of the rules of evidence. Knowledge alone would not be adequate to ensure effective performance: the constable would have to have the skills to identify violations of the law. There would be skills of interrogation, skills in the use of speed detection devices and the examination of the technical aspects of brakes and steering. Finally, to ensure the professional discharge of this work, the constable would need to have the appropriate attitude to the task. This would be shown in the exercise of his discretion either to report the offender or to give a verbal caution, and in his approach and treatment of the offender.

The relative importance of each of the three elements of the task will vary according to the work and these variations will be reflected in the training which staff receive before they are employed on the work. Task analysis is a very important part of the design stage of training courses. Without a statement of the knowledge, skills and attitudes which are necessary for each task, a training course cannot be properly designed or evaluated. In the process of restructuring the sub-division, task analysis is used to build job profiles for the staff to enable them to achieve the required service standards.

The development of the sub-divisional structure started from the point where there was a definition of the standards of a particular service to be delivered and where the component tasks that comprised the service had been identified. Task analysis had determined the knowledge, skills and attitudes that were required to perform the tasks. The next stage is to create a suitable organisational structure by bringing together the people who perform the tasks related to this service. This process is known as establishment review or, in the civil service, as staff inspection.

One of the first levels of analysis for the establishment review is to determine those tasks which must be performed by a police officer and those which can be performed by civilian staff. The next level of analysis will make the distinction between the actual tasks performed to deliver the service and the management tasks of planning, co-ordinating, controlling and monitoring. Both aspects of work have to be considered to determine the qualifications, experience and authority required for each task. These considerations will determine the ranks required to perform the work. On the example sub-division, an analysis of the work of detective constables and detective sergeants might show that there was no distinction between the complexity or seriousness of the crimes they were allocated to investigate. The supervisory activities of sergeants might account for less than 10 per cent of their work. If the level of supervision detective constables were receiving is judged to be adequate, consideration should be given to a reduction in the number of detective sergeants and replacing those officers with detective constables, reducing the amount of investigation work done by the remaining sergeants and increasing the time they spend on supervision and management.

The review will determine those jobs which can be performed by police officers and those which can be performed by civilian staff. The individual tasks will be defined and used to describe the role and responsibilities of the post. Management tasks will be identified and used as the basis for assigning authority levels. At this stage, using the total workload measures, the appropriate numbers of staff can be calculated. The establishment review officer takes these posts as building-bricks and constructs the organisational structure by grouping people performing similar tasks to form sections. Each section will have an appropriate level of supervision and management. The sections will then be built into a departmental structure which will be rationally linked to the force structure.

One of the most important results of an establishment review exercise for the manager is the preparation of job descriptions, which are a basic requirement of proper human resource management. A typical job description will contain the following items:

1   The location of the post, the title and the rank or grade.
2   A statement and description of the job purpose.
3   A list of main duties and responsibilities.
4   A statement of the qualifications and experience that are required on entry to the post.
5   The supervisory responsibility of the post.
6   The supervision to be received by the postholder and by whom the supervision will be given.
7   The contacts the postholder may have with persons inside the force or outside.

By following this process the sub-division will know what is expected by the community, will have defined and measurable standards of service and will have structured staff to deliver service to the required standards. However there is still the important question of how to motivate staff to achieve these standards. One of the important elements of this process is to use the information gained in the service audit, the setting of standards and the task analysis to develop briefing and training material. This process plays a vital part in communicating the purpose behind the work.

The Receipt and Handling of Telephone Calls – the Help Desk Case Study

The typical sub-divisional structure shown in Figure 7.1 has developed in response to the needs of the force looking in on itself, rather than looking out to its customers and designing a structure which responds most effectively to their needs. Of course the existing structures may meet those needs, but it is dangerous to make such an assumption unless there is evidence to support the case. The following example of the problems encountered by telephone callers provides a case study illustrating the need to examine the ways in which the police are responding to needs.

A number of complaints were received by the force about the

service given by a centralised telephone switchboard which covered four sub-divisions for a city and its suburbs. The role of the switchboard was to pass calls to the various extensions at the sub-divisions. The complaints concerned the delay in answering the initial call, delays in the extension being answered and the repeated transfer from one extension to another in an effort to find the required person or someone who would take responsibility for dealing with the person calling. It was clear that the force was not meeting community expectations and there was confirmation from data obtained from the telephone logging computer. This information showed that, over the period of a month, from a total of 81,000 calls, almost 10 per cent of the callers to the switchboard rang off before their call was answered. The service provided by one of the sub-divisional control rooms was even worse, with 26 per cent of the callers ringing off before the call was answered.

Although there was sufficient evidence at the outset to document the failure, there was insufficient evidence to determine the nature of the problem to enable options for solutions to be readily identified. To obtain this evidence a small working group was formed from the people involved in the handling of calls and the first task was for each participant to collect information. A training analyst listened to calls and recorded the actions of the switchboard staff. He found training was not the problem – the staff were being asked to achieve the impossible.

1 There was a relatively small number of calls where it was not easy to determine to whom they should be transferred.
2 Calls passed to an extension for a named person were often transferred back to the switchboard because the person was not on duty.
3 The switchboard operators were spending time connecting internal calls because staff were not using the force internal telephone directory. Almost half the calls to the switchboard were internal, thus reducing the time available for handling calls from the public.
4 Some extensions were not answered although the office was manned; this primarily concerned the sub-divisional control rooms to which calls were passed for officers to be despatched to an incident.

As a consequence of these difficulties it was not uncommon for a switchboard operator to be engaged for upwards of ten minutes in rerouting calls and seeking to gain an acceptance of the responsibility for the call and a message to be taken. Where the switchboard operator consistently received no reply from extensions or a lack of co-operation, the most usual strategy was to route the call to the sub-divisional control room. This had the effect of artificially increasing the workload on the control room, thereby reducing its efficiency and consequently its service.

When messages were taken, the difficulties did not end there because, whilst there was a paper system for recording messages, it was inefficient and, more importantly, was virtually incapable of audit and quality control. An example found by the working group concerned a member of the public who was unable over a period of a month to achieve a satisfactory response from a sub-division because the messages had either gone astray or had been sent for the attention of an officer who was on annual leave. Following the investigation it was clear that no supervisory system existed to ensure that the messages had been acted upon.

Solutions

Increasingly organisations and businesses do not route callers from extension to extension in an attempt to solve the communications problem. Their strategy is based upon one central point for the receipt of information and the provision of advice and help. Where a member of the public required urgent police assistance, they had one all-embracing system, the '999' facility. However, when matters fell outside a requirement for immediate police response, current systems lacked clarity and quality control. In response to this need a centralised interface between the public and the force was established.

The Help Desk was implemented to handle those calls which were falling through the service net. The callers were then provided with a service by the Help Desk resolving their problem, or sufficient information was taken from them to enable their call to be serviced by someone else. If information was taken it was forwarded to the appropriate sub-division or department by fax with a request to contact the caller. If the Help Desk was not informed of the action taken in response to the call, it would speak to the sub-division or the caller again to ensure action was taken. The switchboard and Help Desk also monitored their own performance through set standards of service.

Achievements

As a result of the group's work, a number óf results were achieved:

1   The central switchboard adopted a standard of service – the
    answering of 80 per cent of calls within 30 seconds. On a daily
    basis, the Telecommunications Officer displays the total number
    of calls received during the previous day, the busiest half-hour
    during that 24-hour period, the average time taken to answer all
    calls and the longest and shortest delay experienced on a call.
    This developed a feeling of pride and was therefore a motivating
    factor amongst the staff.
2   The quality of service to the public was improved because a
    further standard was established, which required all calls put
    through to an extension but not answered within 42 seconds to
    be routed from the switchboard to the Help Desk, where they
    were answered immediately.
3   The Help Desk facility also provided an opportunity for manage-
    ment to monitor the quality of call-handling services provided by
    sub-divisions and departments. Sub-divisions and extensions
    which did not routinely respond to calls could be identified and
    information fed back to sub-divisional commanders for appropri-
    ate action.
4   To provide base-line data for future monitoring of public satisfac-
    tion, a public survey procedure was designed and piloted to deter-
    mine public satisfaction with the initial handling of the telephone
    call and the immediate response by the police. This information
    provided a means of auditing the handling service and also a
    mechanism to feed back information to sub-divisional com-
    manders on the quality of service provided by their staff.

*The Role of Organisation and Methods, Task Analysis and Establishment
Review Techniques*

The project which developed the Help Desk started with a simple
problem statement which related to the dissatisfaction of the public
with the telephone-answering and -handling service for non-emer-
gency calls. Public expectations were documented by listening to
callers and listing the types of requests they were making. This
information was supplemented by monitoring the time taken to
answer the call at the switchboard and the requested extension. The
final element in the process of determining how far the service met

community expectations was to use a questionnaire survey of callers to measure their satisfaction.

The solution to the problems associated with the failure to provide a service which met community expectations employed the three basic tools of organisation and methods, task analysis and establishment review. Organisation and methods techniques were used to observe and document the work stages involved in responding to the telephone calls. This process involved examinations of both the human and technical processes. Through this process of documentation the working group was able to identify options to change systems and procedures, introduce additional technology and define the terms of reference for the Help Desk. The analysis also provided a foundation on which standards of service could be defined and measured.

When the pilot study was implemented, police officers were used to staff the Help Desk. During this pilot study records were kept of all calls and from these it was possible, using task analysis techniques, to identify the knowledge, skills and abilities required from the Help Desk staff. It was decided on the basis of this information to create civilian posts to undertake this work. The information from the task analysis was then used to develop job descriptions and the training requirements of the postholders, using establishment review methods. The case study illustrates the importance of gathering information, the benefits of developing organisational change through pilot studies and, finally, the necessity to apply systems analysis and related skills to the development of solutions.

Note

1   A. Campbell, M. Devine and D. Young, *A Sense of Mission*, London: The Economist Books Ltd (1990).

8   Meeting Community Expectations: Achieving the Vision

Some observers of developments in policing could be forgiven for making the point that all too often the police are guilty of imposing solutions to problems which have not been fully defined. The purpose of the fact-finding exercise is to reduce the chances of this happening by documenting information which can be used to plan the way forward. However, unless the process of analysis is structured and disciplined, much of the value of the information can be lost. It is essential to use a framework which will enable the large number of facts to be collated into a form which can provide options for change and, ultimately, the means of measuring the results which are achieved.

The key points of this chapter are:

1 To understand how information is used to determine the current position of the force in the context of the vision of the future.
2 To recognise the role of goals in the analysis of the information to plan the development process.
3 To understand the process of setting goals and the relationship to the corporate plan.

Analysis of the Evidence

The fact-finding process was designed to provide information to respond to the simple question, 'Where are we now?' The process of auditing current services, seeking the views of all staff and documenting community expectations will have produced a wealth of data which have to be processed to determine the answer to the next key question, 'Where do we want to be?' The strength of the process is based on the extensive involvement of staff at all levels and the customers of police services. This principle should extend to the

119

process of analysis. The mechanism for continuing this level of involvement will be a matter for local circumstances, but one option is to convene a conference or workshop with wide representation to make the initial assessment of the data and propose some structure on which to respond to the evidence. The agenda for the meeting would be to consider the following questions:

1   What does the information tell us about our ability to define current levels of service delivery?
2   What does the information tell us about the extent to which current service delivery standards are meeting community expectations?
3   Is the current culture and style of the force promoting excellent service standards or constraining staff in this endeavour?
4   Are current systems and procedures promoting excellent service standards or constraining staff?

What is the Vision?

It is worth recalling at this point the basis on which the fact-finding exercise was started. The Chief Constable, through his statement of intent and corporate plan, signalled his intention to move the force towards one which would base its measurement of success on the extent to which it delivered services which met community expectations. Therefore the answers to the questions on the agenda for the analysis meeting have to be seen in this context. Change is only legitimate where it takes the force one step nearer to the vision. Particularly important are the following:

1   The delivery standards of core services should be matched to community expectations.
2   The culture and style should promote and encourage a sense of common mission and not inhibit it.
3   Systems and procedures should support service delivery standards.
4   Headquarters departments should be perceived as supporting service delivery staff.

Answering the Questions

The meeting will not be able to provide solutions to all the issues raised: in fact it is not the role of this meeting to achieve that end.

The meeting will provide the first comment on the data and propose targets for change. The volume of information will require the meeting to create separate working groups to examine specific areas and report back to the plenary session their opinions on the issues and problems the data have identified. During this first phase the information will take on a sense of order, structured according to the agenda questions. In the second phase, the implications for the problems have to be determined within the context of the vision.

After phases one and two, the information will have some structure and a sense of importance and priority will have been given to the issues and problems. Before the development of solutions can be started, the initial meeting should explore options for action, because there is the opportunity for a broad consensus to be achieved in this representative forum. Finally targets and timescales for developments should be agreed.

The Development Process

To continue the commitment of involvement and to ensure access to a broad range of knowledge and skills, the next phase of the development process should be based on working groups, each taking specific issues and problems to review and develop options for change. These working groups must have a common framework within which to undertake their tasks and to provide a common format for the results. The corporate plan will be the base reference point, and this plan will have contained a broad description of the goals to be achieved in pursuit of the vision in terms of a provisional goal statement. These provisional goals will form the basis of the analysis of the information, but it is possible that new issues will have been identified which did not form part of the original thinking. This is the strength of the fact-finding process. It is likely that these new issues will form the basis of additional goals as the analysis progresses.

The development process can be summarised as:

1 Listing the problems and issues to be considered.
2 Taking each issue or problem and describing in simple terms the desired or ideal state.
3 On the basis of the desired or ideal state, preparing a provisional goal.
4 Against each provisional goal, undertaking an analysis of the

current position and developing outline options for action towards the desired state.

5 Reviewing and revising if necessary the provisional goal and describing development plans to achieve it.

The purpose of goals is to provide more specific direction to police management planners and the managerial link between the corporate plan and objectives. The process involves determining the specific targets which are to be developed from the analysis of the information describing the current state of the force. While the process may seem superficially simple, it is essential to exercise a proper discipline and to undertake the process applying formal rules and procedures. In the absence of such discipline, the results may lack reliability and could undermine the opportunities for achieving substantive results.

A goal is defined as a simple, single-sentence expression which indicates, at a minimum, a result or end state to be achieved. Therefore a goal will always begin with the word 'to', followed by a declaration of a desired result. For example, a simple goal might be (1) to define a service delivery standard for domestic burglaries; (2) to increase the number of detected offences of burglary; or (3) to maintain current delivery standards of handling and managing telephone calls from the public.

There are three types of goals, as the examples above illustrate. The first is an example of a development goal, the second a performance goal, and the third a maintenance goal. The distinction has important consequences for the planning of actions to achieve the goal. Development goals may require a force-wide approach to the analysis and planning, or action by one specific department, whereas the performance goal will probably be confined to actions by staff responsible for service delivery. At a time of change or pressure on resources it is worth considering the use of maintenance goals to ensure that standards of service do not fall.

Thus the task of the working group is to prepare a document which describes how the force will develop from its current state to the desired state. The document will follow a format defining in a simple sentence the ideal state, the goal to be achieved, including a narrative commentary on the options and any qualifying restrictions or constraints which appear to be relevant, which may include a reference to maintaining current performance levels or the constraints imposed by resources.

The Goal-setting Process

It is probably most helpful to conceive goal setting as the discipline of asking a series of questions in sequence, clearly establishing an answer to each question in turn. This method re-emphasises the disciplined planning which is the base of the problem identification and solution process described in Chapter 2. It is likely that some of the questions which will be asked in this process will have been raised in the fact-finding process. If this is the case, the answers given in that stage can be used to assist the preparation of goals.

Question 1   What is the Precise Description of the Problem or Issue?

Whilst this may be apparent from the analysis stage of the fact-finding process, it is essential that the working group review their understanding of the issue and problem, and document it precisely. This step may also identify a number of overlapping issues which will have to be considered separately.

Question 2   What is the Ideal or Desired State?

The process of defining the specific issue or problem in response to question 1 will inevitably have focused attention on the ideal or desired state. However it is important at this early stage of the process to identify to the working group the vision of what they are working towards.

Question 3   What Tells Us We Have a Problem?

The information collected in the fact-finding exercise is the primary source of data to answer this question. The data will identify a range of issues relating to customer satisfaction, the feelings and attitude of staff, and the extent to which current management systems and organisational procedures are inhibiting performance. The response to this question should include some consideration of the importance of specific items because, later in the process, priority may have to be assigned to the most critical issues.

Question 4   Are We Satisfied We Have Sufficient Information Available on Which to Answer Question 3?

Despite the information that has been produced during the fact-finding process, the need for further specific information should not be overlooked. If there are found to be significant shortcomings within the management information system, consideration should be given, if the information cannot be collected in the short term, to specifying development goals which it will be the responsibility of some headquarters support group or sub-divisions to address. The working group has to decide if it can proceed without this information and include it later. If it is unsafe to proceed, the information must be collected and the work of the group temporarily suspended.

Question 5   How Far does the Current Position Fall Short of the Ideal or Desired State?

This is a simple but important question which will identify the performance gap. The answer is the list of factors which have to be changed, or added to current systems or procedures or, in the case of operational issues, improvements in effectiveness. In responding to this question care should be taken not to overlap into listing causes of the failure to achieve the ideal, which is the next but related question.

Question 6   What are the Causes of the Failure to Achieve the Ideal or Desired State?

Having identified the gap between the present and desired states, the causes and reasons for the failure to achieve the ideal must be listed. During this process the benefit of having a working group with members drawn from all sections of the force will be evident. In the first stage of this process no cause should be rejected, however apparently remote. In the second stage of this analysis each identified cause should be examined in turn and tested to determine if it has an impact on performance in the specific context of the problem under consideration.

Question 7   What Options can be Pursued to Achieve the Goal?

In the final stage of the analysis, options for actions will be proposed and examined in detail. At this stage all options should be open because one discounted at this stage might be very attractive in the light of proposals made by another working group who have been exploring a separate but related topic. Each option must be described with the advantages and disadvantages, the costs and benefits and the current constraints, such as staff, equipment, pressure on accommodation and so forth. Where constraints are identified, the working group should exercise their imagination and consider options for overcoming them in the short and medium term.

Working Group Reports

At the conclusion of this process of analysis, the working groups will prepare reports covering each of the issues or problems examined. The report will identify a proposed target in the form of a goal. At this stage the goal will be provisional, to be considered in the context of all the goals proposed by every working group. Each goal will be accompanied by the description of the analysis, which will identify options with the arguments for and against.

It is perhaps helpful at this point to recall the purpose of this whole process. The working group reports contain the answers to the key questions, 'Where are we now?', 'Where do we want to be?' and 'How can we get there?' Unless the reports follow a format which reflects these questions and contains the answers, the process is incomplete. The commitment to a structured and disciplined analysis has been emphasised throughout the process; unless the reports reflect these concerns they will not provide sufficient information on which to make the key decisions about the future steps which will be required to enable the force to meet community expectations.

Ratifying Provisional Goals: Determining the Next Steps

The reports prepared by the working groups will be collated and reviewed, either through the existing policy-making mechanisms, such as a policy advisory group, or a chief officers' group. However, where this process has been specifically employed as part of the Chief Constable's commitment of responding to the challenge of meeting community expectations, an additional mechanism, such as a steering group under the designated chief officer, may prepare a composite document with recommendations for the policy-making forum. Irrespective of the mechanism, the working group reports will be processed to map the way forward. An additional step in this process is to make reference to the group of community representatives described in Chapter 4. Before making any decisions on matters affecting the service delivery, the views of this group should be sought and issues discussed to enable community expectations to influence the decision-making process.

The working party reports will be collated to identify common threads and issues. Where links are established, these issues can be connected and a generic heading used to embrace the related issues. By this process it is possible for many provisional goals to be grouped under as few as ten headings. At this stage the original goals in the corporate plan can be examined to assess the extent to which they are compatible with the broad categories.

Irrespective of the decision-making forum, the issues will be similar, concerned primarily with one question : 'What has to be done to strengthen the ability of the force to meet community expectations?' It is difficult and, perhaps, dangerous to make predictions about the outcome of the fact-finding exercise, but for the purpose of illustration it will be helpful to describe some possible evidence of current problems.

The internal audit of staff will have provided a whole range of issues which are having a negative effect on the quality of services provided. Most common will be the lack of shared mission, with differing views on the same sub-division as to what are the priorities. Equally important will be the extent to which staff 'complain about being overworked'. Policies which require staff to meet service standards are unlikely to succeed unless the staff are convinced that they have sufficient time to meet the standards. The evidence about the culture and management style will produce similar dramatic evidence of the extent to which the force has to achieve some fundamental changes to the approach it takes to creating opportunities for staff to achieve their full potential. On the positive side, this information will show how the same number of staff, with better leadership and organisational structures and procedures, can be significantly more productive.

The service audit will have provided, probably for the first time, objective evidence of what the public expect from the police in any given circumstances and what the police are delivering. In terms of service delivery, there will be information about the specific elements of the service, such as attending the scene, taking statements and providing crime prevention advice but, in addition, there will be information which describes the attitudes, behaviour and style of the police officer's conduct, which form an equally important part of the person's expectations. Key questions for the process of development will be to determine if the force can meet all of the expectations within the current resources and how service delivery standards will be measured in the future. Finally the organisational audit will have identified some of the causes of the failure to meet community expectations because structures and procedures are inappropriate or workloads are too great for the staff available.

Although the various elements of the fact-finding exercise have been examined in isolation, the resolution of the problems inhibiting the force will be a complex amalgamation of many issues drawn from each of these separate areas of analysis. The complexity of the development phase requires the same commitment to disciplined and structured working as the earlier stages. In fact there is probably more danger of the process failing into disrepute at this stage because it is at this point that the eyes of the whole force will be on the process. After several weeks of work and anticipation, there is a general sense of expectation about how soon results will be seen. Unless there is discipline and structure, which includes a determination of goals and timescales, the impetus may be lost and the familiar cry of 'I told you nothing would change' will be heard. Therefore, after the decisions have been made, the force must be told:

1 The goals which have been set for the first phase and the timescales for completion.
2 The process through which these goals will be pursued.
3 Who will be involved in the development process and how it will be undertaken.
4 The benefits for both the community and staff.
5 Which important issues, if any, were not expedited immediately and the reasons for delay.

Making Progress

A factor which should not be overlooked at the start of the development process is the fact that the force has far more information about itself and the community than when the first steps were made to meet community expectations. Furthermore the steps already taken will have created new skills in the staff involved. Therefore not only should the tasks have become more clear, the staff should be more able to undertake the work. At the start of the development phase the role of the co-ordinator is critical. There will be a number of projects to be implemented simultaneously and many will include the issues being considered by more than one project. It is essential to have a formal system of project management to control and advise on progress.

Repeating an earlier point, it would be unwise to be overly prescriptive about the method of developing individual projects, but some examples might assist in illustrating the possible approaches.

Determining Service Delivery Standards for Reported Crimes

Service delivery standards for individual categories of crime will be an inevitable compromise between what the victims expect, what is operationally effective, and what can be achieved within existing resources. The achievement of these standards will involve officers not assigned to sub-divisions, for example scenes of crime officers; it will also raise questions of procedures and organisational structures. For these reasons the project should perhaps be led by the officer in charge of the force criminal investigations. Although the working group report will be available, a further working group to finalise the detail should be considered.

Determining the Support Mandates of Headquarters Departments

The audit of the culture of the force will probably identify a gap between what the staff delivering services expect from headquarters departments and what the latter actually provide. The first step in developing a strong supporting role will be for the departments to produce a document describing their understanding of their role. This will form the basis of consultations with sub-divisions to enable the force to produce an understanding and commitment from departments describing their contribution to the meeting of community expectations.

In some cases, for example control room staff and scenes of crime officers, these departments provide a direct service to the public. In such cases it will be necessary for these departments to have defined standards of service which form the basis of a contract with sub-divisions. For example, where there was a complaint to a sub-division about a delay in response to a call in the control room, or the arrival of the scenes of crime officers, the sub-divisional commander could refer to the service standards and determine if the department had met their target. In the absence of such contracts, the sub-division is being held accountable for an element of the service which it does not control.

The involvement of many elements of the force perhaps favours the use of a co-ordinator at chief officer level, but with a working group dealing with the detail.

Improving Internal Quality of Service

It is likely that this issue will cover more than one goal, for example the submission of files or the cleanliness of police cars. Experience in other organisations demonstrates the significant improvements in productivity which can be made by doing a task once but doing it right. Where standards exist for files and so forth, the process of development can best be achieved in the workplace with progress being monitored and reported to the co-ordinator at regular intervals. It is essential for the process to be formalised because simply exhorting staff to 'do better' is unlikely to succeed. Poor quality is often associated with lack of commitment at all levels, excess workload, inefficient procedures and ineffective quality assurance mechanisms. Unless the problem is confronted in all its symptoms temporary improvements may be followed by a rapid regression to the former state.

Staff Providing Services Feeling Isolated from Information Sources

The staff audit will provide information about the quality of internal communications and this will provide a base-line from which improvements can be measured. Improving communications will have many facets, from training of staff with management responsibilities to the development of internal newsletters and briefing sheets.

Traditionally the press and public relations departments have directed their attention to external marketing, but the need for internal communications should be a matter of increasing concern. To make progress in this area the department could be given responsibility for devising a strategy to improve internal communications.

Matching Workload to Resources

This is another topic which will probably be covered by a number of goals. Initially there will be a need to provide core services to the standards which have been agreed within existing resources. In these cases the task will be to match demands to the staff available and possibly make proposals to redeploy staff to these key areas. However in the medium term it will be sensible to plan alternative, more efficient working methods to free resources to meet any anticipated increase in demands. The immediate needs may be met by forming a working group from sub-divisional staff to design a formula to deploy staff in response to current workloads. To plan for the future it may require the management services department to research the problem and prepare options to respond to anticipated increases in work. Planning for the future reassures service delivery staff of the continuing commitment to meeting community expectations.

The examples which have been briefly described are intended simply to illustrate some options for taking the development process forward to achieve results. They are necessarily simple because, in the absence of the information which would be available in the actual process, it is unwise to speculate about the most appropriate mechanisms to move from the analysis of the information to the achievement of the goal. However the following items are critical factors in the process:

1   The process must be co-ordinated at chief officer level.
2   The fact-finding exercise must be disciplined and structured.
3   The production of reports analysing the issues must follow a common format and include a statement of the desired future state in the form of provisional goals.
4   When the provisional goals have been agreed, a formal project-planning system must be used to develop the action required to achieve the goal.
5   There are a range of formats and systems which can be used to achieve the goals, which include working groups, co-ordinated action by individual departments or sub-divisions, or formal research projects.
6   The development process must be disciplined within a set time-scale to focus attention on the importance of the process and to underwrite the continuing commitment to meeting community expectations.

The Corporate Plan Revisited

At this point it is worth recalling the discussion about the development of the corporate plan in Chapter 4. It was suggested that a corporate plan should be drafted to provide a base for the process which would be initiated to ensure that the force was in a position to deliver services meeting community expectations. Following the fact-finding exercise, the force will now be far more knowledgeable about all aspects of its services and the expectations of the community. Therefore it makes sense to re-examine the corporate plan and revise it. In particular the tentative goals which were proposed as part of it should be amended in line with the goals which have been defined in the process of analysing the information.

Before leaving the corporate plan it is worth considering the question of its future. Without overstating the point, the reason for the force engaging in this extensive process of self-examination and customer consultation was the extent of ignorance about some basic facts critical to the successful delivery of services. A sensible leader would try to ensure that mechanisms would be put in place to collect key information which would in turn ensure that service delivery standards in the future met community expectations. Therefore the force must adopt a strategic planning system which collects key information relevant to service delivery standards, has mechanisms for anticipating demands, uses working groups drawing service delivery staff into the process of developing policy proposals and uses formal disciplined systems, including the setting of goals to direct the process of meeting community expectations. The basic concepts were described in Chapter 2 in the context of the management cycle. The force should not lose sight of the vision of the ideal police organisation which was described in Chapter 3. Without something to aim for, it is not surprising how easily police forces lose direction and arrive at unintended destinations.

Community Problem Solving

Three types of goal have been described. The focus has been directed towards development goals because of the extent to which the force will have to change its culture and style to achieve the vision. These changes will establish delivery standards for a range of core services. In Chapter 3, the concept of community problem solving was raised as one of the core services. The diversity of community problems makes the definition of service delivery standards more difficult to achieve, so it is essential to use the structured system of problem identification and action planning to resolve the problems and measure the results. The basic anchor point for this process will be the performance goals established through the fact-finding process. In addition to describing organisational developments, community concerns will have been documented and formulated into either a general goal concerning quality of life in the community or more than one goal reflecting concern about specific issues such as dwelling-house burglaries, disorderly behaviour by young people, or road safety.

These goals will have been developed through the process of fact finding, but the means of achieving them requires a more structured approach to operational police planning than is generally the case. The framework for the sub-divisional response is based on the policing by objectives model described in Chapter 3. In the next two chapters the setting of sub-divisional objectives and action plans as the means of solving community problems is described in detail.

9   Community Problem Solving: Setting Objectives

For the purpose of clarity and to assist management effectiveness, a distinction has been made between the core services and the concept of community problem solving. The former are concerned with responding to individual or specific requests for assistance or a service; the latter form the basis of longer-term actions which will result in a permanent solution to the problem being experienced by the community. Historically police forces have been less effective in dealing with these persistent community problems, adopting 'one off' response tactics, rather than developing a coherent approach to deal with the underlying causes. In this section, the policing by objectives methods will be used to develop a framework for community problem solving using a system of objectives, action plans and evaluation techniques.

The key points of this chapter are:

1   To understand the purpose and definition of objectives.
2   To be able to define a measurable result.
3   To understand the process of setting objectives.
4   To understand the role of provisional action plans.

The Purpose and Definition of Objectives

In the fact-finding process, evidence will have been collected which shows in general terms the extent to which community problems are creating a lack of confidence in the police. The issues which will have been identified will cover traditional issues such as crime, road safety and traffic regulation and social order and tranquillity. It is possible that the force will have embraced all these issues within one goal, such as 'to improve the quality of life in the community'. Alternatively goals may have been written to direct attention to specific issues such as crime and public tranquillity. In any event, the sub-divisions with their primary responsibility for service delivery will be required to respond to these expressions of public concern to improve the quality of life in neighbourhoods.

Force goals will have a relevance to every sub-division, but there will be differences between sub-divisions in the extent of public concern over specific problems. For example, the pattern and frequency of road accidents may vary throughout the force. It is equally likely that the capacity for police to influence and thereby reduce the number of road accidents will also vary between sub-divisions. The sub-divisional commander must use his knowledge and skills to identify those problems which are causing the greatest concern and develop a response. This process involves the full range of management skills within the disciplined structure of the policing by objectives model. There is nothing in the PBO model which requires police officers to achieve miracles, or indeed to achieve the impossible. Policing by objectives requires police managers to analyse their problems and direct resources at solving them, working from a realistic assessment of the likely results to be achieved.

An objective is linked to a goal; its purpose is to allow sub-divisional superintendents to analyse their own particular problems within the context of force-wide goals and, having made the analysis, to adopt objectives in an order of priority which reflects the needs of their communities and the capacity to respond to those problems. Objectives are thus the link between goals and action plans. Their purpose is to describe *what* is going to be achieved and *when*, and the timescale against which those results are going to be measured.

An objective can be defined as a single-sentence statement of a specific, measurable result to be achieved within a given time period. When an objective is written it must identify a *specific measurable result*. If an objective is not capable of being measured, it is not possible to determine whether the problem being addressed has become more or less serious during the period under review. An objective must also specify the *time period* during which it is to run. Once again this is essential for the evaluation process.

When an objective is written, the question should be asked, 'If I achieve this objective, what will it contribute to achieving a goal?' It is possible to write an objective which addresses a specific problem on the sub-division and subsequently results in a solution, without contributing to the achievement of a goal. If that is the prospect and there are limited resources on the sub-division, then it may not be appropriate to pursue such an objective because it is not reflected in the corporate priorities of the force.

The definition of an objective refers specifically to performance objectives. However, just as there are maintenance and development goals, it is possible to define maintenance and development objectives. For example, a sub-divisional commander may be concerned that the quality of police response to emergency calls could become reduced through diverting resources into other activities. He may therefore write a maintenance objective with a view to preserving the standards of service which have been defined in force policy.

During the action planning consultations which lead to the formulation of objectives, it may be apparent that there are insufficient sources of data on the sub-division to identify a specific problem. In these circumstances it may be necessary to define a development objective which directs all or some of the staff on the sub-division to produce better information towards identifying that specific problem. Performance objectives could then be defined when the information becomes available.

The Measurable Result

An objective must specify, in measurable terms, a result which is to be achieved. In some cases measurement can be relatively straightforward; for example, if the number of burglaries in dwellings is known, then any change in the number gives a direct measure of a result. In reality such direct measures are not easy to identify as there may be a number of factors affecting the rate at which burglaries are reported. However such factors do not prevent these direct measures being employed, providing they are used in the circumstances described below.

The direct measures are called quantifiable objectives in PBO, but of equal importance are qualitative objectives. A qualitative objective is used where the force is endeavouring to improve the quality of the service it provides to the community. Such a qualitative objective might be 'to improve the satisfaction of telephone callers to the sub-division in 1992'. It is apparent that the measurement of such an objective is not easy, but the use of a carefully constructed questionnaire survey of callers at the beginning of the year and later would provide measures of satisfaction.

The necessity to measure qualitative objectives can be illustrated by reference to reports which have been written in the past concerning community policing. In several of these reports the reader can find various objectives which are written to describe the purpose of introducing a specific community policing project. However, when the reader turns to the section concerned with evaluation, if indeed such a section exists, it is difficult, and often impossible, to determine the real measurable results which have been achieved in terms of solving community problems. In some instances substantial claims are made for the success of such schemes, claims based upon virtually no evidence apart from subjective and anecdotal references.

Objectives should only be written if they are made in response to some specific problem which has been identified on the sub-division. If this problem has been identified and exists in reality, rather than in the imagination of a well-meaning police manager, the evidence that disclosed the problem can be used as an *indicator* to develop a measure of improvements. For example, public dissatisfaction with the police may be indicated by the results of a social survey which shows that the public are unhappy about the attitude taken by officers when responding to calls for help. The public might also be dissatisfied with the failure of police officers to communicate the result of enquiries or cases to witnesses and complainants. Letters may be received which criticise officers for being discourteous when reporting motorists for traffic offences. Complaints may be received from the public who state that, when they telephone their local police station, 'the telephone rings for several minutes before it is answered'.

The range of issues can run from the relatively serious to the minor or trivial. However, if a force examines its relations with the community, there are a number of indicators which may suggest there are problems to be addressed in terms of enhancing public satisfaction with the service they receive. When a qualitative objective is written it can specify the particular areas requiring attention in action plans, and it will be those indicators capable of measurement which can then be used to establish an improvement in public satisfaction with the quality of police services. No one indicator should be used on its own, and it is recommended that at least three indicators are employed as measures to determine performance in respect of a qualitative objective.

The Objective-setting Process

Who Sets Objectives?

The sub-division will have the specific responsibility for setting objectives. Depending on the management philosophy and structure, the superintendent may have to submit the objectives to a chief superintendent for confirmation. The process of setting objectives, however, relies upon the 'top down', 'bottom up' planning process. With this procedure superintendents will consult throughout the sub-division, and each level within the sub-division will have a responsibility for communicating ideas up through the structure to the superintendent. It is preferable for a sub-divisional group to be established in which all ranks and departments are involved; it could be this forum which consults throughout the sub-division, before sitting together to define finally those objectives which will be accepted by the sub-divisional commander. There is no right or wrong way in which this consultation should take place, providing it does take place. For the purpose of the exercises given below, the consultation group will be called the Sub-divisional Planning Group.

How Will the Objectives be Set?

In the goal-setting process described in the preceding chapter, it was suggested that those involved should ask themselves a series of questions in a specific sequence. Having answered a question, they can then move on to the next stage. It is recommended in the consultation process which takes place to set objectives that a similar question and answer format should be adopted.

Having received the goal statement and the corporate plan from the Chief Officer Group, each goal should be examined in turn to establish exactly how it relates to the sub-division and the problems being experienced by the community.

Before taking specific examples of goals and translating them into objectives, the process can be described in the abstract by going through the series of questions and answers. This process should be undertaken for each of the goals, where there is more than one general goal related to community problems. Where the goal is written in general terms to embrace a wide range of community problems, the sub-division can prepare a preliminary list of community problems and issues which have been highlighted through the community consultation process and should then use the question and answer format to consider each issue in turn. Figure 9.1 provides a format to assist the process.

WORKSHEET

1 GOAL

2 DESCRIPTION OF THE PROBLEM
(stating sources of information and indicators/measures)

3 ADDITIONAL INFORMATION REQUIREMENTS

4 POSSIBLE STRATEGIES
(provisional action plans)

5 RESULTS MEASUREMENT
(performance indicators)

6 OFFICERS INVOLVED AND RESPONSIBILITIES

7 RESOURCES AVAILABLE

8 PROVISIONAL OBJECTIVE

9 PRIORITY RATING

Figure 9.1   Provisional objectives

Question 1   In Terms of the Goal, What Specific Problems are We Experiencing on This Sub-division?

If, for example, the goal in question relates to a reduction in the number of burglaries, it must be asked if this is a problem relevant to the sub-division. If so, to what parts of the sub-division is it a problem and, more specifically, what exactly is the nature of the problem? In order to answer these questions it will be necessary to make a careful analysis of current management information. It is possible of course that this process will highlight deficiencies. Should this happen it may preclude a detailed analysis of the problem at this stage, and steps will have to be taken to remedy the deficiency before an objective can be proposed.

If the Sub-divisional Planning Group is satisfied it has sufficient information to answer this question, it can proceed to Question 2.

Question 2   Given the Scope and Nature of the Problem, What Can We Do on This Sub-division to Solve the Problem?

An essential component of any objective is to determine what is going to be achieved in a given time period. For example, are we going to reduce burglaries by 5 per cent, 10 per cent or by an even more ambitious proportion? Setting the target for an objective can never be an exact science, but the distance which the leap of faith must make in determining the target can be significantly reduced, first, by the quality of the analysis undertaken in response to Question 1 and, second, by a careful consideration of the possible methods which could be applied to solve the problem.

Therefore, although action plans will be discussed in more detail in the next chapter, at this stage it is necessary to consider provisional action plans, and here as many ideas as possible should be obtained on the sub-division and considered, analysed and assessed. It would not be appropriate at this stage to undertake detailed action planning, but the Sub-divisional Planning Group should ensure they have the resources to carry out a proposed action plan. They should consider the cost/benefits of prospective action plans, the degree of support required from other sections of the force, such as the traffic department, any special skills or training which may be required and any additional equipment which will be necessary to carry through the action plan.

Having considered the nature of the problem and discussed what could possibly be done to solve it, the subsequent evaluation has to be considered.

Question 3   How Will We Know We have Achieved our Objective; What Measures Will We Use?

Once again we turn to the critical and difficult issue of measurement. Measures of police effectiveness have been elusive in the past but the method of analysis and planning which is fundamental to the problem-identification process identifies things that can be measured. To answer Question 1, the analysis undertaken to identify the exact nature of the problem will have involved some indicators which can form the basis of measurements of effectiveness. For example, in the case of burglary, the number of crimes reported in a given period will form part of the measurement process.

It is essential at this stage of the planning process to consider the measurement of objectives, failing which the whole system could become discredited – considerable effort mounted to address an objective could be effort wasted if it is impossible to determine whether it made any difference to the size of the problem.

The setting of objectives will usually be the responsibility of the sub-divisional superintendent. The process will inevitably involve consultation throughout the sub-division but, in the implementation stage, some delegation to specific members of the sub-division will be essential for action plans to be pursued. Thus, at this stage, it is important to ask the next question.

Question 4   Who Will be Responsible for Writing Action Plans to Achieve this Objective?

It is necessary at this stage of the planning process to establish individual responsibilities on the sub-division. Whilst all members of the sub-division will have some level of responsibility for action plans, the planning, implementation, co-ordination and evaluation of specific action plans can be a major task. Therefore it is essential to avoid defining a range of objectives which will place an undue burden in subsequent action planning on one or two members of the sub-division. If this appears likely, then a number of alternatives should be considered. As an example, the load could be spread between other officers who do not have the primary skills but would be capable of carrying the action plan through; alternatively other work could be delegated further down the structure to leave the individual with more time to perform the additional duties. It may even be necessary for objectives in that particular area to be reduced, on the grounds that there is insufficient time for officers to co-ordinate and evaluate the action plans. These considerations bring us to the next question.

Question 5   What Resources are Available?

The major, yet often neglected, primary resource on the sub-division is the man-hours available to meet all the duties, responsibilities and functions required of the sub-division. The measurement of time and, more specifically, the amount of discretionary time which is available on the sub-division, is a crucial prerequisite. As far as first-line personnel are concerned – uniformed patrol officers and detective constables – it is essential to establish that they have discretionary time available before being given additional work to perform in connection with action plans. Similar considerations are necessary for other ranks within the sub-division who are being given additional functions, such as the planning, implementation, co-ordination and evaluation of action plans.

This aspect was discussed under the previous question but it cannot be over-emphasised. If, say, a detective inspector is being made responsible for the implementation of a specific action plan directed towards crime control, then it is essential to establish clearly that he has sufficient discretionary time in which to plan, co-ordinate and evaluate the action plan. If such time is not available, this matter has to be confronted and solved before any further demands can be made on the officer's time. When an assessment has been made of the resources available, the final question in the planning process can be asked.

Question 6   *What are the Priorities of the Sub-division?*

The question is most appropriately asked after all the goals have been considered and the process described above has been undertaken for each goal in turn. A sub-division would be very fortunate if it had sufficient manpower resources to undertake a number of action plans directed towards every goal. Therefore some mechanism has to exist to determine priorities. The principal concern of the sub-division is to meet community expectations. In this context it would be appropriate to consult the community in the process of determining priorities. By taking this step, the sub-division would provide further evidence of its commitment to the community; consultation would also provide an opportunity to explain the limitations of resources. If there were subsequent complaints of police inaction in connection with community problems the consultation process over priorities would provide a reference point to counter any unjust criticism.

Setting Objectives : A Case Study

For the purpose of this exercise we will assume two goals have been formulated by the Chief Officer Group: to reduce the amount of suppressible crime; and to enhance public tranquillity. We will now deal with the objective-setting process in respect of each goal. The procedure described below should not be interpreted as the only means by which this process can be undertaken, but rather as one method which may be appropriate to the particular circumstances.

It should also be understood this is a *brief* guide, and does not attempt to cover all the issues that may arise in the process of defining sub-divisional objectives.

Goal 1   *To Reduce the Amount of Suppressible Crime*

On receiving the goal statement from headquarters, the sub-divisional commander requests an analysis of the current crime situation on the sub-division from the detective inspector and the local intelligence officer. He asks for papers to be prepared for discussion by the Sub-divisional Planning Group at its first meeting to consider the sub-division's objectives.

At the initial meeting of the Sub-divisional Planning Group it is established, from the analysis undertaken, that the most significant change in crime patterns during the last three years is a substantial increase in the number of reported burglaries. There appears to have been no additional population influx which could have accounted for this increase, and it is agreed by the Planning Group that a reduction in the increase of burglaries in dwelling houses should be examined as a possible objective for the coming year.

At this stage ideas are floated as to possible explanations for the increase in burglary. The detective inspector and local intelligence officer are given the task of preparing a more detailed analysis of the burglary pattern on the sub-division, the type of property being stolen, the type of houses which are being attacked, the time of day of offences, any information on the disposal of stolen property, and intelligence concerning the persons who have been arrested and admitted offences of burglary.

At the following meeting of the Sub-divisional Planning Group it is established that two distinct burglary patterns exist on the sub-division. The first pattern relates almost exclusively to a municipal housing estate and houses adjoining. Here properties are being attacked during the daytime, between 10.00 am and 4.00 pm, when cash and small carry-away items such as portable radios, jewellery and so forth are being stolen. It has been found from detected offences that juveniles appear to be responsible for the majority of these crimes, and the property is either being sold or exchanged at schools or being disposed of in local second-hand shops.

The second burglary pattern is more difficult to determine but appears to be the work of more professional burglars, who are attacking carefully-selected houses and stealing relatively high-value property such as televisions, videos, stereos and the like. The sources of disposal of this property are not readily identifiable. The Sub-divisional Planning Group agrees that the first pattern of burglary, which is apparently the work of juveniles, is a matter which can be addressed on the basis of the present information. However the group members also agree that the second pattern of burglary requires more detailed analysis, information and intelligence before action plans can be proposed.

Members of the Sub-divisional Planning Group are then asked to consult officers throughout the sub-division, with a view to their proposing possible action plans which could be used to combat the problem of juvenile burglaries. We have now reached the stage where the question concerning problem identification has been asked and answered. We are now posing the question, 'What can we on the sub-division do to find a solution to the problem?' (Question 2).

At a subsequent meeting of the Sub-divisional Planning Group, a number of provisional action plans are suggested by the members. These can be listed as follows:

1 Following the analysis of the burglaries believed to have been the responsibility of juveniles, a reduction of truancy from local secondary schools is proposed as a means of reducing them. By reducing the number of potential burglars in the neighbourhood, at times when houses are most likely to be unoccupied, the number of burglaries is likely to be reduced. The strategy would involve police officers paying particular attention to young people of school age seen out of school during school hours. This plan, it is suggested, would have a deterrent effect on juveniles who are truanting from school. Second, it would provide a basis of intelligence which may establish a pattern of truanting amongst the most severe offenders. Third, it might establish patterns of associates which could be used if a juvenile was arrested for burglary and his associates were known and suspected of being involved.

2 Local publicity to ask members of the public to report young people who are seen hanging around the street during school hours in suspicious circumstances. This, too, would have a deterrent effect on the juveniles. Second, it would highlight the problem of burglary for the community, thus encouraging citizens to take more care of their property; and third, it should greatly enhance the volume of information coming to the police and therefore increase the likelihood of a crime in progress being detected.

3 Liaison with local schools, which should ensure that they are aware of the police concern with juvenile crime in the area. It might also make them more aware of the truancy problem and encourage them to take steps to assist the police in reducing truancy. Finally it might also generate a deterrent effect by publicising the police strategy in schools. School teachers could also be encouraged to assist the police by reporting instances where property is brought into the school for the apparent purpose of being traded between pupils.

4 More frequent visits to second-hand dealers' premises. This strategy might discourage unscrupulous dealers from trading with juveniles, or alert and encourage them to report instances where young people attempt to sell the type of property being stolen from houses.

The Sub-divisional Planning Group accepts all the provisional action plans as possible methods which could be implemented. The Group's next concern is to establish what measures will be used to determine whether these action plans are achieving tangible results if implemented. The overall measure to be used, termed the *primary measure*, will be the number of reported burglaries in dwelling houses over a specified period. This decision is made as it has been established, through the victim survey section of a social survey conducted in the community, that more than 90 per cent of all burglaries in dwelling houses are reported to the police.

Whilst these figures will form a basis for determining whether the objective has been achieved or not, there are other measures which may be helpful in identifying the effectiveness of specific action plans. Therefore *secondary measures* must be adopted.

The detailed analysis undertaken on the sub-division has already suggested measures of effectiveness. It is possible to keep a record of, and therefore count, the number of juveniles who are seen out of school between 10.00 am and 4.00 pm It may be possible to obtain, with the co-operation of schools, a count of the number of unexplained absences from school both before the action plan is implemented and during its implementation. The impact of the publicity campaign encouraging members of the public to report suspicious incidents to the police can be evaluated by the number of calls received from the public. Furthermore the number of arrests made for crime directly following calls from the public can also be measured before and during the action planning period. Similarly it is possible to count the number and frequency of visits to second-hand dealers, the number of occasions on which dealers report suspicious transactions to the police and the number of persons who are arrested as a result of these calls.

Although a reduction in the number of reported burglaries will indicate a successful achievement of the objective, it is equally important to determine which, if any, of the action plans contributed to achieving the objective. For example, if virtually no property is sold by juvenile housebreakers to second-hand dealers, then the action plan of regularly visiting second-hand dealers may be an activity which should be discontinued.

It should also be recognised that this process of evaluation is enhancing the overall fund of knowledge the sub-division has about the way it performs its function. Over the years it may develop and store a range of action plans to counter specific problems which, having been solved, arise again at some later time. At this stage of setting provisional action plans, however, the Sub-divisional Planning Group is only required to ensure that there are measures available to be used should these action plans be adopted.

During the process described, some duties and responsibilities have already been assigned. For example, the superintendent has been exercising his role as the person responsible for ultimately defining the objectives. Similarly the detective inspector and local intelligence officer have been involved in problem analysis. At this point, however, it is helpful to use the provisional action plans proposed previously, as a means of identifying those officers who will have direct responsibility for implementation, co-ordination and evaluation.

It is unnecessary to describe all the roles that have been outlined in the provisional action plans, but it can be seen that the uniformed patrol officers will have a major responsibility for the observation of juveniles of school age on the streets during school hours. It will be a matter for the superintendent's judgement as to who should undertake the school liaison role and, finally, it is likely the detective inspector or the local intelligence officer will have a role in evaluating the consequences and impact of these action plans.

It has been emphasised that there is a critical requirement within PBO to establish the amount of time available for action plans. In some cases existing data may not provide action planners with an accurate assessment of the amount of time available. However it should be possible to make some reasonable estimates of this time. It is equally possible that some action plans will require little, if any, dedicated time; that is, substantial portions of specifically allocated time. For example, the observation and contact with persons on the street is an everyday activity of uniformed patrol officers and therefore the proposed action plan is not in the least innovative. What is important in respect of the action plan is that the activities will be directed towards specific target areas and, furthermore, the results of those activities will be evaluated. Thus, as well as establishing the amount of time available for action plans, it is equally important, at the stage of provisional action planning, to make some realistic estimates of the number of man-hours that will be consumed in those action plans by the various officers who are involved.

As a result of the analysis carried out on the sub-division, it is established that 25 per cent of all burglaries reported during the previous year were committed between 10.00 am and 4.00 pm From the detection figures and an analysis of the modus operandi (MO) it is estimated that the majority of these burglaries were committed by juveniles. It is anticipated that the proposed action plans could reduce these crimes by half. Accordingly, it is decided to set an objective: to reduce the rate of burglary in dwelling houses on the sub-division by 10 per cent in 1992. The objective is then considered in the context of other objectives to determine its priority for the purpose of allocating resources. In some cases, depending on the management structure, there may be an additional stage of referring the objective to the divisional chief superintendent or the co-ordinator at headquarters before it can be ratified.

Goal 2   To Enhance Public Tranquillity

Goal 1, which addressed the reduction of suppressible crimes, was very obviously a performance goal which led to the development of a *quantifiable performance objective*. The second goal emphasises the qualitative aspects of the community problem solving and thus we will be looking towards defining a *qualitative performance objective*. However the strategy adopted will be identical to that undertaken in defining the quantifiable performance objective.

The first step taken by the sub-divisional superintendent on receiving Goal 1, was to call upon the services of the detective inspector and local intelligence officer to analyse the current position using historical data. With Goal 2, the sub-divisional superintendent may be in the best position to assess the nature and scope of the problem in relation to public tranquillity. He may be the officer who is a regular visitor at public meetings and the meetings of various residents' and community associations. He may also be responsible for answering letters of complaint from members of the public who are concerned about noise in their area, incidents of drunkenness and so forth. Therefore the sub-divisional commander may be a person with key information in respect of this goal. However, even if this is the case, it is likely that other members of the sub-division, for example area constables, will have some knowledge of matters which affect feelings of public tranquillity. For the purposes of this exercise, we will confine the examination to problems that have been identified on a large municipal housing estate.

When the Sub-divisional Planning Group meets, it is established that, during the previous year on this housing estate, complaints have been received from members of the public and the residents' association concerning the following matters:

1 Incidents of drunkenness and rowdiness outside the two public houses on the estate, mainly at closing time.
2 Vandalism to publicly-owned property, in particular telephone kiosks and bus shelters.
3 Defacing of walls and other amenities on the estate by the use of spray paint.
4 Noise and speeding by youths on motor-cycles.
5 The local youth club has been the focus of a number of complaints concerning noise, litter and vandalism in the adjoining area.

As a result of its discussions, the Sub-divisional Planning Group members are not only aware of the scope and nature of the problem, but they are also able to relate the problem to specific sites within the housing estate: the public houses, youth club and public amenities, such as telephone kiosks, bus shelters and so on. There is ample evidence of a problem, and the next issue concerns action plans to solve some, if not all, of the various aspects to the problem.

At a subsequent meeting of the Sub-divisional Planning Group, a number of action plans are proposed:

1 Use of directed patrol by uniformed officers who will position themselves at known trouble spots at relevant times in an attempt to deter offences or, if necessary, enforce laws in relation to drunkenness and public order. This plan would involve officers attending the public houses at closing time, or parking the police car in a prominent position outside the youth club at relevant times, and so forth.
2 Observations on specific known targets of vandalism. Here sur-

veillance could be carried out either entirely by police officers or with the support of technical aids such as television cameras or night vision equipment.

3   Specific enforcement of traffic laws in relation to motor-cyclists, having particular regard to licensing and insurance legislation, and the Construction and Use Regulations relating to exhaust systems.

4   Liaison with the youth club. This could take a variety of forms, such as attending the youth club to give advice to the members and management concerning the nuisance apparently being caused in the locality. It might be thought appropriate for a police officer to become a member of the management committee but, more importantly, it may be useful for the police to encourage local residents to become members of the committee, in order that their viewpoint may be communicated directly to the young people.

5   Liaison could be established with the local bus company, British Telecom, shopkeepers, the Parks and Gardens Department and local publicans in order to introduce improved means of identifying trouble spots when they arise.

When pursuing a qualitative objective, it is all too easy to assume that activities will necessarily produce results. For example, there has been a trend in recent years to presume that police involvement with youth clubs will automatically produce tangible, beneficial results. This may or may not be so, but such benefits cannot be assumed and, before the police become involved in the committees of youth clubs, they should be sure of the results they are trying to achieve. Similarly it is important not to confuse some quantifiable results with necessarily bringing an improvement in terms of the original problem.

It would be preferable to have no complaints of noise or disorderly conduct outside public houses, rather than an impressive record of arrests for public order and drunkenness offences. However such data should not be disregarded. Although arrests may be made outside public houses this may not result in fewer complaints from citizens. Therefore other strategies may need to be adopted. For example, a more positive supervision of the public houses themselves to reduce under-age drinking or other problems may, in fact, be more effective in reducing complaints than arrests made outside on the car park.

In the final analysis, the indicators that will tell us whether or not we have made some impact on this goal will be public opinion and perception of any improvements in public tranquillity in the neighbourhood. Therefore, when we come to establish the measures of determining the achievement of an objective, it will be necessary to identify at least three measures to provide an answer to the question.

Once again, the examination and analysis of the specific problem produced a number of potential measures. To illustrate, the volume of letters of complaint received from residents' associations and community groups, the number of complaints from individual citizens concerning noisy motor-cycles and the number of complaints from the bus company or British Telecom concerning damage to their property are all measures of the results of police activities.

By this stage in the process, the Sub-divisional Planning Group has identified a specific problem, has considered the means by which the problem might be solved, and has established performance measures which can be used to determine the degree to which the objective has been achieved. By going through this process, the Group has suggested possible strategies in terms of provisional action plans. It is now appropriate to discuss who will be responsible for writing action plans when the objective becomes operational.

In the discussions concerning Goal 1, which related to addressing suppressible crime, the specimen objective concerned the whole sub-division and involved a number of officers in action planning, both in uniform and CID, and at a number of different ranks. In the case of Goal 2, the objective is related to specific problems concerning an individual housing estate. This housing estate will be on a beat patrolled by an area constable. If this officer's full potential is to be developed and used, he could be conceived as a 'beat manager' and made responsible for co-ordinating all police activities on the beat. If this position was accepted then it would be appropriate for the area constable to be responsible for the preparation of action plans. Should the proposal be agreed, this would add status and credibility to the role. Additionally, and equally as important from a management viewpoint, it would place responsibilities upon an officer who has an intimate knowledge of the problems of the area and who, furthermore, is likely to have a professional commitment towards finding the solution to those problems.

Before we leave the planning process, the availability of resources must once again be discussed. Some of the action plans that have been proposed can be carried out in the normal course of patrol, but observations of specific targets to detect vandalism will require the specific allocation of time. Also the directed patrol of potential trouble spots must be accorded the same status as attending a call from the public. After all, it would be self-defeating if an officer, in carrying through an action plan, stationed his vehicle in a prominent position overlooking a public house car park or the youth club and after five minutes was directed elsewhere to attend a call from a member of the public. If directed patrol is adopted as an action plan tactic, then this must include safeguards to ensure that officers do in fact implement the action plan and not merely go through the motions.

Following the discussions by the Sub-divisional Planning Group and the review of provisional action plans, an objective can be written to cover the issue of public tranquillity on this housing estate. The objective is written as follows: to improve the public's perception of public tranquillity on housing estate X during the next year. As this is a qualitative performance objective, it will also contain performance measures, as specified below:

1   There will be a reduction in the number of letters of complaint received from residents' associations and community groups in the next year.
2   The number of incidents of damage to public property and amenities will be reduced during the next year.
3   There will be a reduction in the number of complaints from members of the public concerning drunkenness and rowdiness outside public houses on the estate during the next year.

Confirmation of Objectives

After the sub-divisional commander has considered all the force goals and is satisfied the community's needs and anxieties have been considered in the process of drafting objectives, the process of documenting the results of the planning stage can be completed. It is important to develop standard formats for the documentation and an example of a proposed format is shown in the provisional objectives worksheet in Figure 9.1. The headings follow the questioning sequence which is described on the pages following the figure. The use of this format will produce a standard approach to the setting of objectives and provide the necessary background information to explain the context in which it was set. To support the summary contained in the worksheet there should be a narrative description of the background to the objective and specific reference to the community's concerns about the problem it is seeking to resolve. This description will assist in the process of determining priorities among objectives competing for resources and provide information to people outside the sub-division who may have a responsibility in the objective-setting process. When preparing this documentation it is useful to check the contents to ensure that the following questions have been answered. Unless all the points have been covered, staff who have to respond to the objective by taking actions will not be fully briefed as to the context and the extent to which the objective is a response to community expectations.

1   How is the objective linked to the goal?
2   Will achieving the objective contribute to achieving the goal?
3   What is the nature of the problem on the sub-division as expressed by community expectations of the police?
4   Are the conclusions which have been drawn from the analysis reasonable?
5   Have steps been taken to assess the resource requirements?
6   Are there resources available?
7   What measures are to be used to establish the results?
8   Is the objective realistic, in so far as it will be challenging to the participants but not impossible to attain?

The final stage of the objective-setting process is to confirm the objective and assign it a priority. The nature of this process will depend on local management policy; for example, it may be a matter for the sub-divisional commander's own decision, but in other cases reference may have to be made to a divisional chief superintendent or headquarters. Irrespective of the process, it is essential to have some means of communicating with the community involved and to reassure them about the actions which will be taken to resolve their problem. Setting objectives is not an end in itself; it is a process committed to community problem solving.

10 Community Problem Solving: Action Planning

[handwritten: How problems expressed by community will be solved. Solution to problems.]

The development and implementation of action plans is the fourth step in the policing by objectives model. By following the structured and disciplined approach to identifying and analysing community problems, the final stage of taking action is more likely to be effective. The structure of the process also enables the Chief Constable to delegate responsibility for decision making with more confidence.

During the process of setting objectives described in Chapter 9, provisional action plans have been suggested, as this is the only practical manner in which the system can be carried out. However, whilst a wider degree of discretion will be allowed in the action-planning process, if there is one single key to the successful implementation of PBO it will be the skill with which sub-divisions can undertake the preparation, co-ordination and measurement of action plans.

It is possible, at this stage of the PBO model, to lose sight of its central purpose. That purpose is to *solve community problems*, and *not to be overwhelmed* in a paper-chase where every single activity undertaken on the sub-division must be preceded by a written action plan. Such an outcome is not an inevitable and automatic consequence of adopting PBO; in fact it is worth recalling the central component of the model, which is to perform only those police activities which can be demonstrated to produce some tangible and beneficial result. If an avalanche of paper does accompany the adoption of policing by objectives, it should be understood that this is not the fault of the PBO model, but is due to a lack of understanding and commitment to the underlying concepts. The danger will be discussed later in this chapter.

The key points of this chapter are as follows:

1 To understand the value of action plans as a means of providing

153

direction and structure to the day-to-day policing activities of officers.

2   To understand the place of action plans in the PBO cycle.

3   To understand the criteria which must be applied to action plans when a choice is being made between them.

4   To understand the need to establish the roles and responsibilities of officers in relation to action plans.

5   To be able to apply the criteria to action plans to choose the most appropriate policing method.

6   To understand the distinction between primary and secondary measures and their use.

Action planning brings the process right down to the constable on the beat and therefore it is worth pausing to ask some questions about the benefits the management process can bring to operational officers. To adopt a process such as PBO requires the active commitment of all officers and they are entitled to ask why they should be committed and what benefits they will receive. In fact when constables are introduced to this system of management they may simply ask, 'What is so different about policing by objectives?'

The question raises a number of key issues in relation to policing by objectives, and it is worth asking further supplementary questions and inviting the reader to reflect upon the answers based upon his or her own experience of police work. The first question is simple, 'In the past have you been aware of the force policy concerning the prevention and detection of crime, enforcement of road traffic law, enhancement of public tranquillity and so forth?' It is all too easy to make assumptions about these critical issues based upon some vague definition handed down by Rowan and Mayne. But can these vague concepts really help in determining in the minds of individual officers the priorities they should be pursuing to serve the needs of the community?

This brings us to the second question, which is equally important: 'Do I always know why I am performing a particular aspect of police work?' In connection with answering calls for service, dealing with demonstrations and other straightforward matters, this question is not too difficult to answer. But in relation to the more routine and everyday activities, such as the enforcement of road traffic laws, reassurance patrolling, visits to schools and so on, is it always clear exactly what this work contributes to the meeting of community expectations?

Even if an officer does know why he is performing a range of police activities, he may not be able to answer the question, 'Do I know what I have achieved as a result of these activities?' It has been shown that a significant contribution to job satisfaction is giving an employee information reflecting the results he achieves from his work.

Finally, even if an individual is aware of what he is achieving, there is the further question: 'Do my supervisors know what I am achieving?' Criticisms have been levelled at staff appraisal systems but it is not the concept of staff appraisal which is usually at fault. It is more likely that the person making the appraisal has extreme difficulty in giving an objective assessment and evaluation of an officer's performance. This fact is not a criticism of individual police supervisors, but more a consequence of a management system which has not, in the past, been very good at clearly determining the results of individual effort.

These issues were raised in Chapter 5, and were included in the fact-finding exercise. Unless these legitimate questions and concerns can be answered a commitment to excellent service to the public is unlikely to be achieved or sustained. By adopting PBO as a management model, the Chief Constable has prepared a corporate plan which is available to every member of the force, who should therefore share a sense of common mission by being made fully aware of the overall direction and policies of the force. This general policy directive has been followed by a set of goals which establish priority areas for police action, and should ensure a more co-ordinated and forthright attitude towards pursuing the policy determined by the Chief Constable. These broad policy directives prompt, at sub-divisional level, an analysis of the problems being expressed by the community and an outline of options to pursue solutions. This sub-divisional analysis will involve all staff; thus they will not only be contributing to the design of the solutions to problems, but they will also be consulted on why these problems need to be the subject of police efforts. Therefore staff throughout the force should have a clear knowledge of the overall vision of the future direction of the force, the goals and, furthermore, they should have a good working knowledge of the problems being experienced by the community on their sub-division.

When action plans are prepared and implemented individual members of staff should have a precise awareness as to why they are carrying out particular activities and the results they are expecting to achieve, together with a clear understanding of their individual responsibilities and how these fit into the overall strategy.

The aspect of PBO which makes it radically different from previous management innovations in the police is the absolute commitment to measuring and evaluating results. By undertaking this measurement and evaluation strategy, not only will the force be in a position to determine the results it has achieved, but individual officers will also be able to establish their achievements and be held accountable and rewarded for those achievements. Therefore, to return to the question, 'What is so different about PBO?' the answer lies, not in the individual component parts of the model, but in the way in which all elements are brought together in a coherent and co-ordinated process which leads from broad policy to action on the streets and subsequent evaluation.

Action Planning Procedure

The action plan is the final step in the planning stage. It serves as a direct instruction to staff to perform certain tasks related to a given objective, which will be evaluated by specific predetermined measures. Any action plan must satisfy two basic tests: first, it must be reasonably likely to achieve the desired result; second, it can be pursued by the staff who are proposing to use it. If an action plan fails on these two criteria it should be rejected and alternatives proposed. If the process described so far has been followed to this stage, it is very unlikely that a proposed action plan will fail the standard tests as, in the objective-setting stage, provisional action plans have already been proposed and tentatively agreed by the sub-divisional superintendent.

The action-planning procedure at this stage of PBO is mainly concerned with making choices between alternatives, assigning specific responsibilities for the various parts of the action plan and establishing time periods at which evaluations will occur.

Choosing Options

In the preceding chapter a number of provisional action plans were proposed for illustration. When this stage of the process is reached in practice, it is likely that there will be many more provisional action plans than the number set out in the examples. The difficulty of choosing between action plans will be related to the number which are available. Whatever choice is made, providing the choice has been made upon sound grounds, it cannot be open to criticism, as it is the sub-division's responsibility to manage their resources at this stage of the PBO process.

To assist in making these choices it may be useful to assess each provisional action plan against a checklist of criteria:

1 *Cost – benefits* A primary reason for changing policing strategy is the desire to improve the service to the community. Therefore all action plans must be carefully examined to establish if they are an effective use of resources and, of equal importance, whether the use of resources will be efficient. By efficient we mean that there may be a number of ways of achieving a given objective, but our responsibility as managers of scarce resources is to ensure we achieve the objective with the least cost. To take a very simple example, a particular action plan may require 16 man-hours a day to carry out. This time could be found from within existing duty time, or it may be necessary to employ officers on overtime. If it is only possible to find the resources by using overtime, then so be it, but, if a more careful use of resources enables the same task to be performed in duty time without incurring additional costs, this latter strategy must be more efficient.

This first criterion will require a careful consideration of all the cost implications of the action plan. In cases where special equipment is needed, the costing is relatively straightforward to calculate. But in cases where man-hours are the significant cost it should be remembered that this involves not merely the man-hours which will be used to carry through the action plan, but also those man-hours required in planning the strategy, the co-ordination and monitoring, and possibly other factors such as additional training for officers.

Unfortunately the costing of police services, particularly where precise cost data are not available, is a difficult task, but it is something to be borne in mind throughout this process. In many instances it may be possible to give only broad estimates of costs, but even this is better than no consideration at all being given to this very important management matter.

2 *Range of activity* The sub-division, or the unit within the sub-division proposing the action plan, must be capable of carrying it through on its own. The action plans which were proposed in the previous section were all assumed to be, and indeed were, capable of being performed by sub-divisional resources.

However an action plan related to improving road safety could involve a widespread publicity campaign concerning the dangers of drinking, and warning motorists that particular attention would be paid to this offence in the coming months by the officers on a specific sub-division. Whilst this strategy may well produce the desired results, a sub-divisional commander would need to ask himself if it is appropriate for him, as an individual, to undertake an action plan which has obvious ramifications beyond the boundaries of his sub-division. This does not mean such an action plan should automatically be dismissed as an option, but it is something which might be considered at force level as more appropriate as a common action plan across the force area, and additional to sub-divisional action plans.

3   *Additional support*   When considering the range of activities above, managers were cautioned against actions going beyond their sub-divisional boundaries. Here we are concerned with requests for additional support from specialist departments to assist operations within the sub-division. It is important to consider the possibility of obtaining additional support from specialist officers at the earliest possible stage in the action-planning process. If this is not done, it is possible that such support may not be available. If the support cannot be given by resources off the sub-division, then the action plan may have to be radically altered at this early juncture, or abandoned altogether. In the 'bottom-up' consultation which takes place in the planning process, the requirements for specialist support should be identified at an early stage and communicated through the planning system to the co-ordinating department at headquarters.

4   *Preparation and development*   In some cases action plans can commence immediately they are formulated, but in other instances there will be a need to undertake a period of preparation and development before the plan can be implemented. The requirements for preparation and development must be carefully considered, as it is very damaging to arrange for manpower to be available on a particular date in order to proceed with an action plan, only to find the necessary preparation has not been done in advance and the plan has to be postponed.

5   *The effects on other police efforts*   One of the more difficult tasks of the police manager is to attempt to predict the likely effect of a course of action on other areas of police activity. These implications are twofold: first, those for the police organisation – that is, internal implications – and second, those for the community – external implications.

A simple example of internal implications is where an action plan requires a number of officers to perform certain activities at a particular time, which means as a consequence that these officers are not available to do duty elsewhere. Thus, if area constables are encouraged to be involved in youth activities, then the same officers, during the hours they are in youth clubs and schools, will not be providing a visible presence on the street. Therefore, when it comes to assessing the impact of patrolling officers on the perceptions of police visibility by the public, the fact that officers spend many hours inside youth clubs and schools must be a consideration when the results are being assessed.

To take another example of police involvement with youth, a policy of greater contact between young people and area constables may provide benefits and gains to the police image, but these could be eliminated entirely by an action plan which required strict enforcement of road traffic regulations in respect of young people riding motor-cycles.

In most cases action plans will have implications either internally or externally, or both, and it is not being suggested here that such action plans should automatically be discarded. Far from it, as it is likely that a carefully managed action plan which appears to have conflicting implications may simultaneously produce successful outcomes. However this is only likely to occur if the wider implications of such action plans have been considered from the outset and steps have been taken to minimise the possible conflict between them.

6 *Special or additional skills* Where action plans will require special or additional skills, these must be identified at an early stage and either the skills must be provided within a sub-division by 'on-the-job' training, or a request must be made to the training department for assistance and co-operation. A simple example would be where an action plan involves uniformed patrol officers undertaking crime prevention surveys in houses in an effort to reduce the opportunities for burglary. It is likely that the officers undertaking these surveys, if they are to be conducted in a professional manner, will require some form of crime prevention survey training. Thus it is a prerequisite of the action plan that this training be provided before it can proceed.

7 *Equipment requirements* In many cases equipment either will be or can be made available on the sub-division, but this aspect must not be overlooked. For example, if night vision equipment is not available to pursue an action plan involving evening obser-

vations of areas being subjected to vandalism, then the action plan may not be undertaken.

8　*Manpower resources*　The critical issue of manpower availability has been stressed at length. If manpower is not available for action plans then they simply cannot be executed. There are two general ways in which manpower can be made available. First, having established the amount of discretionary time available to uniformed patrol officers, a number of officers can be detached from uniformed patrol duties to perform specific tasks in a small squad. However it must be remembered that sufficient manpower resources must remain within the unit, to carry out those tasks which are designated as essential activities and to maintain service delivery standards. Thus, under this strategy, if the discretionary time of a unit of officers is 50 per cent, it may be possible to reduce the discretionary time of some officers to 20 per cent and thereby release officers for alternative work, but this will mean that the remaining officers will have to work harder.

The second strategy is to start to fill those periods of discretionary time with specific activity. This is what typically occurs at present, where officers who are not responding to calls or otherwise engaged will patrol potential trouble spots on foot or check cars for crime or road traffic offences, and generally perform those tasks which are called self-initiated. The action-planning strategy would not radically change this mode of operation. However it would attempt to ensure that all these self-initiated activities undertaken by officers from time to time are directed towards specific objectives, and therefore every activity would be channelled towards some measurable and achievable results. This is known as *directed patrol*.[1]

The proposed action plans in respect of burglary discussed in the preceding chapter involve both these strategies. For example, during discretionary time, officers could direct their attention towards young people on the street who appeared to be absent from school. The plan to visit second-hand dealers, however, could involve detaching two men from uniformed patrol duties and having them working in plain clothes. Whichever strategy is chosen, it must be remembered that PBO is not a process for getting 'blood out of a stone'. If there simply is not the time available to perform action plans, then they should not be implemented.

In previous chapters a question and answer approach was suggested as a very useful way of dealing with the issues raised by particular aspects of PBO, and the strategy of choosing options is no exception. Thus we can summarise all the preceding points in the following questions:

1 Will the action plan be effective and is it the most cost-effective means of achieving the desired result?
2 Does the range of activity proposed by the action plan extend beyond sub-divisional boundaries, or is it outside the scope of activities normally associated with the duties of the officers involved?
3 Does this action plan require support from specialist departments at headquarters?
4 Does the plan require a period of preparation or development before it can be implemented?
5 Will the proposed action plan have an impact on other police activities and, if so, what are the consequences of this impact? Are they tolerable or do they make the action plan inappropriate?
6 Does the action plan require special or additional skills and, therefore, training for the officers of this sub-division?
7 Does the proposed action plan involve any additional equipment and, if so, will it be, or can it be made, available?
8 Are there sufficient manpower resources to carry through this action plan?

Establishing Roles and Responsibilities

At this point we are concerned with who will do what and when. During the period of analysis which accompanied the setting of provisional action plans, responsibilities have already been assigned. For example, in matters relating to crime, the detective inspector and/or the local intelligence officer may have been involved. The area of action having been established, the person to have responsibility for overseeing implementation must be decided. Here it is possible the responsibility may change from detectives to the uniformed officers if the action plan involves uniformed personnel. Thus implementation may be under the general direction of a uniformed inspector.

During implementation it will be necessary to monitor each action plan and subsequently to provide an evaluation. This could be done by the person responsible for implementation, or it may be appropriate to return the evaluation process to the officer who made the original analysis, as he has a more detailed knowledge of the broad aspects of the particular problem. There exists a considerable degree of flexibility as to who should perform these tasks, but it is essential the specific roles are all assigned. Accordingly every action plan will have an officer responsible for the analysis and definition of the problem, preparation of the detailed action plan, overseeing the implementation, providing the day-to-day monitoring and producing the final evaluation report. In some cases it may be that one individual officer will have all these responsibilities; in most cases it is likely several members of staff will be involved at various stages.

Throughout this process, the sub-divisional commander will be involved in ensuring the component steps are undertaken and that the officers are competent to perform them. The sub-divisional superintendent will be responsible for the final review of these action plans and the preparation of the sub-divisional evaluation report.

Action Planning: A Case Study

After the Sub-divisional Planning Group had made a detailed review of the crime problem on the sub-division in response to the force goal 'to reduce the amount of suppressible crime', the following objective was defined: to reduce the rate of burglary in dwelling houses on the sub-division by 10 per cent in 1992. In the process of developing this objective, four provisional action plans were proposed, which can be briefly described as follows:

1   Special attention by uniformed officers to juveniles of school age who are seen out of school in school hours. This will be known as the Truancy Project.
2   Publicity asking members of the public to report young people loitering in streets in suspicious circumstances. This action plan will be known as Publicity.
3   School liaison to explain the problem of juvenile crime in the area with particular reference to burglaries, accompanied by a request to enlist the aid of schools to reduce truancy and report instances where suspected stolen property is being traded between pupils. This will be known as Schools Liaison.
4   Regular checks on second-hand dealers to trace and recover stolen property. This will be known as Dealer Checks.

The process of choosing options is one of comparisons. All the above action plans seem likely to produce some positive results but it is worth comparing the cost, the benefits and all the additional questions in relation to these plans before settling for one or more action plans.

Such comparisons in police work can never be an exact science. A simple matrix grid may help to clarify thoughts and make the choice a more objective process (see Figure 10.1). Across the top of the page, the four action plans are presented. Down the left-hand side of the grid are shown the eight specific questions which it was suggested should be asked in comparing action plans. The first row relates to cost and benefits and, under this item, we are most concerned with the likelihood of the plan producing the desired result. To illustrate this, and to assist with comparisons, a scale of 1 to 4 is proposed where a score of 1 equals 'very *unlikely* to achieve the result' and a score of 4 equals 'very *likely* to achieve the result'.

The second row, Activity Range, can usually be answered 'Yes' or 'No': 'Yes' would indicate that the activity is one which can realistically be confined to the sub-division and be implemented without interference with other sub-divisions; 'No' would indicate that the plan will certainly spill over onto adjoining sub-divisions or, perhaps, the force area as a whole.

The next five rows, which are headed Specialist Support, Preparation/Development, Adverse Effects on other action plans, Special/Additional Skills and Equipment, can all be answered on the same scale, again ranging from 1 to 4, but, in this case, a score of 1 would equal 'a *great deal* of this in the action plan', whilst 4 would indicate '*none* of this in the action plan'. Thus, when considering specialist support for the Truancy Project, it is clear that this is not required, and therefore a score of 4, meaning 'there is no need for specialist support in this action plan', can be assigned to this aspect of the plan.

The final row concerns the man-hour resources required. It is not the purpose at this stage to assign specific man-hours to these action plans, although it may be desirable at some time. However at this point a decision can be made as to whether the action plan will be performed in the discretionary part of normal patrol time or be carried out using separate manpower, either by drawing from units on the sub-division, or by reducing the discretionary time of uniformed patrol officers by taking away some of their number to perform separate duties.

For this case study we will briefly examine each of the action plans

COMPARISON WORKSHEET

	TRUANCY PROJECT	PUBLICITY	SCHOOLS LIAISON	DEALER CHECKS
Costs/benefits 1 = v. unlikely 4 = v. likely	4	3	3	3
Activity range Yes = confined to sub-div No = extends beyond sub-div	Yes	Depends on the medium chosen	Yes	Yes
Specialist support	4	4	4	4
Preparation/development	2	4	4	2
Adverse Effects on Other APs	2	4	4	4
Special/additional Skills	4	4	4	2
Equipment required	3	4	4	3
Time NP = normal patrol SM = separate manpower	NP	NONE	NP	SM
TOTAL	19	23	23	18

Figure 10.1   Action plans

proposed during the objective-setting process to show how these comparisons can be made.

Truancy Project

The strong evidence of the involvement of juveniles in housebreaking, particularly during daytime hours, encouraged the Sub-divisional Planning Group to believe activity by uniformed patrol officers would both deter juveniles from committing burglaries and raise the possibility of increasing detection through the checking of youths who had been involved in such crimes. In these circumstances it is believed that the action plan is very likely to achieve the required result, and therefore, in the first row, it is given the score of 4.

It is believed that this is an activity which can be performed on the sub-division without encroaching on other areas of the force. Therefore its activity range is appropriate, and it is marked 'Yes' in that row. Specialist support is not required for implementation, and therefore it scores 4, but there will be some limited preparation or development, as the local intelligence officer will be required to establish an index of juveniles who are found truanting from school. He will need to keep particular records of juveniles who are found to be involved in committing offences of burglary, and he will be required to prepare material to brief uniformed officers on crime patterns and so forth. Therefore, to indicate some preparation for the action plan, it is scored 2 in that row.

It is possible that the action plan could have some adverse affects on police relations with young people, therefore a score of 2 is again given against this element. As far as additional or special skills are concerned, these are not thought to be required in this case and a score of 4 is allocated. A very limited amount of equipment is going to be needed by the local intelligence officer and this, it is believed, can be made available, so a score of 3 is given. Finally the manpower resources are to be drawn from normal patrol time and this is indicated by marking 'NP' in that row.

On the comparison criteria used it can be seen that the action plan is believed to have a very good chance of reducing the amount of burglary on the sub-division; it is specific and can be contained within the sub-division. It also appears to be very cost-efficient, as it can be carried out during normal patrol activity.

Publicity

If a deterrent effect can be demonstrated by the use of publicity which encourages law-abiding citizens to report suspicious incidents to the police and, simultaneously, encourages potential juvenile criminals to believe they may be reported to the police by concerned citizens if they are seen acting suspiciously near houses, then this action plan has some likelihood of achieving the result. Therefore a score of 3 has been assigned under this heading.

The activity range of this action plan will depend to a certain extent on the type of media which is used for the publicity. If it is confined to local newspapers, then it is possible the activity could be limited to the sub-division, but if, for example, the local radio is involved, this action plan will have an influence beyond the sub-divisional boundary. In view of these circumstances, an answer has not been given in this row, but it has been noted that it 'depends upon the media used'.

It has been assessed that there will be no need for specialist support, no requirement for preparation or development, there will be no adverse effects on other action plans, and additional skills and additional equipment will not be required; the action plan will not necessitate any time allocation from operational officers, as the briefing can be done by the sub-divisional superintendent in the course of his normal media briefings. Consequently each of these headings receives a score of 4.

To summarise, this action plan has little or no cost implications to the sub-division in terms of manpower. The likelihood of it achieving results is difficult to assess immediately, but if there is a good public response then the possibility of being reported by concerned citizens might well deter potential juvenile burglars from committing these crimes.

Schools Liaison

Once again, the amount of support received from the schools, and the deterrent effect which might be accrued from this support, is difficult to estimate at the outset.

However it is known from previous dealings with schools in the area that they are more than likely to co-operate, at least in a limited way, and therefore it can be reasonably believed this action plan is likely to achieve the desired results. For these reasons it is given a score of 3. This is a matter that can be dealt with exclusively on the sub-division, therefore the answer to the question concerning activity range is 'Yes'. The action plan will not require specialist support, preparation or development; it should not have any adverse effects on other action plans, it will not require additional skills or training, and no additional equipment will be required. It can also be performed during normal patrol time by area constables who, in their course of duty, visit schools.

This action plan will not incur additional manpower costs on the sub-division and, although its exact effects are difficult to predict at this stage, it is very strongly linked to the Truancy Project action plan. Some additional benefits may be accrued from this Schools Liaison action plan as a direct spin-off from the Truancy Project action plan. Indeed, it could be seen they complemented each other.

Dealer Checks

Regular checks with dealers may lead to the recovery of stolen property and the identification of those persons responsible for its theft, which in turn may stop those people committing further offences. An additional effect of this action plan could be to deter burglars from taking their property to the second-hand dealers for disposal, or at least to make such transactions difficult. What cannot be assessed, of course, is the extent to which these crimes will still occur and other means used to dispose of property. It cannot be said categorically, therefore, that this action plan will be very likely to achieve results, but, equally, it is unlikely that it will not achieve some results. A score of 3 under this heading would seem appropriate.

This is an activity which can be confined to the sub-division, although there is the possibility the action plan may displace the disposal of stolen property to second-hand dealers to other areas of the force. The action plan will not require any specialist support (score 4). The officers who are making the dealer checks will need to be aware of the description of property recently stolen, and this information will have to be extracted from crime reports and collated locally. This will require some preparation and background work to check up on recent crimes before the plan can be set in motion. In recognition of this development need, a score of 2 has been assigned under this heading. It is believed this action plan will not have an adverse effect on other action plans, and it is therefore given a score of 4.

The officers who undertake responsibility for executing this action plan will require some training to prepare them for the task, for example as to the means of identifying property through serial numbers and the like, the records dealers maintain and the force policy and statutory authorities related to the seizure of property believed to be the subject of crime. To indicate this training need, a score of 2 has been assigned. There will be a limited requirement for additional equipment for the maintenance of certain indices and other records, and a score of 3 has been assigned under this heading.

Having considered the necessity for a detailed knowledge of property recently stolen, the need for officers to get to know second-hand dealers, and the requirement of a consistent policy concerning the procedure for recovering stolen property, it is thought appropriate to give the execution of this action plan to two officers on a full-time basis. Thus there is a need for separate manpower to be allocated, and this has been indicated in the last row.

To summarise, it is believed that this action plan will lead to the recovery of stolen property, which may produce detection of the persons responsible for its theft. However it is likely that this action plan will increase detection rather than produce a reduction in the absolute number of burglaries being committed. Further, it is likely property from other crimes, such as thefts from motor vehicles, will also be involved in the action plan. This particular plan is the most expensive one in terms of manpower, as it requires a separate manpower allocation.

Making the Choice

The foregoing may at first sight appear to be a very laborious and unnecessary process, but it has only been used here in a relatively simple example to illustrate the concepts and procedures. In reality there might be a number of action plans under consideration and it is only through this proper comparison that their relative strengths and weaknesses can be assessed. In making the final choice for action plans, the two most important criteria will be the likelihood of achieving a satisfactory result and, second, the cost in terms of manpower to be used. On these two criteria, the Truancy Project is the most attractive. It has, on the analysis, the most likely chance of achieving the desired result and it is an activity which can be carried out at very low cost.

Publicity and Schools Liaison depend very much for their success on the co-operation of the public generally and schools in particular. The fourth action plan concerning dealers should be seriously considered, but this activity may be more appropriately combined with other crime action plans, providing they are to the benefit of the sub-division, for example plans relating to thefts from motor vehicles and the like. This fourth action plan is the most expensive in terms of manpower and also involves setting up yet another specialist squad, albeit of only two officers, which once again removes an opportunity from the general uniformed patrol officer to become involved in the implementation of action plans.

It is decided after these considerations that the sub-division will implement the Truancy Project action plan. The process of preparing the action plan prior to implementation, assigning responsibility for the various parts of the action plan to individual officers and determining the evaluation measures is shown in Figure 10.2, which identifies the objective – to reduce the rate of burglary in dwelling houses by 10 per cent in 1992. This is followed by a brief narrative comprising the action plan title and description. The action plan clearly shows units involved. The tasks which must be undertaken include a briefing of the officers involved. The local intelligence officer will be responsible for preparing the index and collating information obtained by officers. Area constables will be responsible for informing the schools in their area that the police will be taking particular interest in young people who appear to be absent from school without reason. The final task shown is the major activity, which is the observation of juveniles on the street during school hours.

Figure 10.2 should be seen as a summary of the constituent elements of the action plan. The effective communication of the plan to the staff involved in its execution is critical to success, therefore it will be necessary to produce a detailed document for this purpose. The familiar format of operation orders using Information, Intention, Method, Administration and Communications as headings should be considered for this task. The importance of briefing staff cannot be overstated. The sub-divisional commander should ensure that all officers fully understand their roles and responsibilities and, in particular, that officers are given instructions as to how to implement the action plans to ensure no adverse comments against police procedures. Area constables must be fully aware of the superintendent's policy before they can inform schools to make sure that there are no misunderstandings and good relations between the schools and police are maintained. It will also be necessary to indicate to uniformed patrol officers the way in which any checks of young people are to be conducted and recorded. Care must be taken to ensure no damage is caused to relations between police and young people.

[handwritten margin note:] must not damage police + young people relationship.

OBJECTIVE
To reduce the rate of burglary in dwelling houses by 10 per cent in 1992

ACTION PLAN TITLE AND DESCRIPTION
Truancy patrol
To conduct spot checks on juveniles of school age during school hours with a view to determining whether they are authorised to be absent from school

UNITS INVOLVED

Sub-divisional
Uniformed patrol officer
Area constable
Local intelligence officer

Others (i.e. HQ)
None

MAJOR TASKS

Preparation
Brief officers
Brief local intelligence officer
Prepare index and collate the number of checks carried out
Inform schools

Execution
Carry out checks on juveniles during school hours

RESULTS MANAGEMENT
Primary measure
Number of relevant offences of burglary reported

Secondary measures
Number of target juveniles checked
Number of juveniles truanting from school
Number of burglaries detected

CO-ORDINATOR
Sub-divisional chief inspector

REVIEW PERIODS
Four-weekly

Figure 10.2   Summary of chosen action plan

Figure 10.2 also identifies, under the heading of Results Management, the measures to be used to evaluate the results of this police method. The *primary measure* will be the number of offences of burglary reported during the target hours. But it is equally important to provide information on a number of supplementary indicators, such as the number of target juveniles seen or checked, the number of juveniles actually truanting from school (a figure which will have to be obtained in co-operation with the schools) and the number of burglaries detected as a result of the action plan. These are the *secondary measures*.

A distinction has been made between primary and secondary measures because they tend to serve different purposes. The primary measure will always be linked directly to the objective, and is the primary evaluation criterion. Secondary measures are usually one step removed from the objective, as they measure things which on their own do not establish the achievement of the objective, but measure contributions to the achievement. The primary measure is used to establish whether progress has been made towards the objective; the secondary measures should help to establish *why* or *how* the desired results have or have not been achieved.

From the outset it must be clearly stated who will have responsibility for co-ordinating the action plan; in this case, responsibility has been assigned to the sub-divisional chief inspector. Finally, review periods will need to be established and, as school terms are of a limited length, it is proposed that the action plan should be subject to a four-weekly review to determine its results.

It was mentioned in the introduction to the action planning section that there was a danger of becoming overwhelmed by the paper recording of action plans and associated matters. This is not an inevitable consequence of policing by objectives and is something to be avoided. However the action plan is the key to the policing by objectives process and it is the one thing, above everything else, that will provide the base for the successful evaluation of the efforts of the force to establish the extent to which community expectations are being met through improvements to the quality of life in neighbourhoods. Therefore, given the critical nature of action planning in relation to the overall policy of the force, time spent on the administration of action plans must be considered as a valuable contribution to improving the confidence the public has in the commitment of the police to responding effectively to their needs.

The use of an action-planning document such as the one shown in Figure 10.2 is recommended, and a proper recording procedure should be introduced to enable action plans to be co-ordinated and monitored in a professional manner. It is a matter for individuals whether this recommendation is accepted but, in the final analysis, it will be the responsibility of the person making the decision to ensure he is in a position to provide a sufficiently detailed evaluation to support any claims of success in achieving results.

Note

1   J. R. Howlett, S. H. Killman and J. B. Hinson, 'Managing Patrol Operations', *The Police Chief* 34–43 (December 1981).

11 Community Problem Solving: Achieving and Measuring Results

In the preceding chapters the policing by objectives process has moved from the corporate plan (step 1) to goals (step 2), followed by objectives (step 3) from which action plans were prepared (step 4). These four steps are concerned with planning and organising resources, and the reader might be forgiven for wondering why this complex planning process has been undertaken if, as an end result, we are going to implement a plan which involves amongst other things paying special attention to juveniles found in the street during school hours. On a superficial examination, this may indeed seem to be a very long and laborious process to arrive at a point which has been visited on many occasions before by police officers attempting to control crime.

To emphasise the importance of the planning process it is worth making the following observations which, to some extent, were covered in the introduction to action planning. The PBO process does not require radical changes in the way police officers do their job on the street. However, when the PBO process is adopted, constables should be able to stop to reflect on the principles underlying the activities they are performing, and they should be aware of the following matters:

1 They should know how any particular police activity fits into the overall mission of the force as it strives to meet community expectations.
2 They should know exactly what their contribution will be to this mission.
3 They should know who is responsible for co-ordinating the activities and evaluating the results.
4 They should know the results they, as individuals and the group of officers to which they belong, are achieving.

5 They should know that, if there are no benefits being achieved from a particular activity, it will be changed or abandoned.

If they have this greater degree of knowledge then they should certainly feel part of a team, and therefore gain greater satisfaction from the work they do. Furthermore the force should be infinitely more effective in its pursuit of the mission, as it will not contain a number of individuals all doing 'their own thing', but will gain strength from the co-ordinated efforts of staff who share a common purpose.

The key points of this chapter are:

1 To understand the place of the implementation process in the management cycle.
2 To recognise the factors to be addressed in the day-to-day management of the implementation of action plans.
3 To understand the functions of the evaluation stage in the management cycle.
4 To recognise the difference between tactical and strategic evaluation.
5 To be able to recognise and apply various methods of evaluation.
6 To understand the considerations implicit in deciding the time-scales of evaluations.
7 To be able to apply the checklist of criteria which must be used to evaluate action plans.
8 To understand the specific requirements of the evaluation of development goals.
9 To understand the requirements of the annual review process and the issues to be included in the evaluation reports.

If there is a radical difference in the implementation stage of the PBO cycle, then it relates to the ability of officers to understand why they are doing certain things. For example, a management directive which merely tells officers to 'get out and do a bit of traffic law enforcement' or instructs area constables to 'get involved in the local community' is a far cry from the careful analysis of problems on the sub-division, the involvement of staff at all levels in identifying strategies which may lead to solutions, and a subsequent careful and co-ordinated programme of implementation and evaluation. This may entail officers reporting motorists for traffic offences or area constables being involved in youth activities in schools, and thus the 'actions on the street' may well be identical, but the management philosophy which is directing them is substantially different. It is the lack of coherent management practice which is causing the police to fail in their efforts to maintain public confidence. If the police cannot measure the quality or effectiveness of their work, it is impossible to counter criticisms from the public.

There are dangers in being deceived into believing that the implementation process under PBO is similar to the more traditional forms of police management. As far as individual officers are concerned, their key responsibility will be to ensure the effective and efficient management of their own time, and this is a matter which all staff, regardless of length of service or post, must make their guiding management principle. It is no longer sufficient for any staff to tell their supervisor they are 'busy' unless they can also show the supervisor exactly what results they are achieving. It must be remembered that police activities have no value in and of themselves; they must be judged by the *results* they achieve.

Day-to-Day Management of Implementation

The extremely diverse nature of police work on the one hand creates an interesting and challenging management task, but, on the other, makes it very difficult to provide instruction to managers which will cover every foreseeable eventuality. However it is important to establish the structure and procedures to be used when implementing action plans. Random modifications to action plans must be avoided by establishing methods to make changes. Staff must be motivated and committed to the plans. Systems for recording the essential elements of the plan must be designed and adopted. In some cases action plans will have implications for other aspects of police work. These must be co-ordinated by establishing appropriate procedures to prevent disruptions to the plans or existing working arrangements. Finally, the force must understand the role of monitoring as a learning, rather than a punishment-centred exercise.

Modifications to Action Plans

Experience of executing an action plan may reveal, sooner or later, matters that have not been anticipated, thereby necessitating modification or amendment to parts of the action plan. Any such adjustments should not be made by individuals, but a system should be established whereby these problems can be dealt with by the officer responsible for co-ordinating the action plan. It will be his decision to make changes during the course of executing the action plan.

If the preparation for action planning has been done with sufficient care, major alterations to the plan should not be necessary. There are dangers in making day-to-day modifications to a plan which is fundamentally sound, as the end result of these changes could affect the plan to such a degree that it becomes unworkable.

Motivation

Any person who has been involved in changes at work is aware that initial enthusiasm and motivation can decline with the passage of time, with performance returning to the level which may have existed before the change took place. This must not be allowed to occur. There is always the possibility of staff feeling that merely going through the motions is all that is required and that, providing all the parts of the process appear to be carried out, this will be sufficient. In some cases, this may well be true but, should this occur, it will be a criticism of the way in which objectives and action plans have been formulated. If the objectives can be achieved with little or no effort then they have not been formulated in a sufficiently challenging way. This would not be a criticism of PBO, but a comment upon the way in which police managers have been more involved in rather than *committed to* the process.

Recording

In concluding the action-planning section, a caution was given concerning the use of written action plans and the way in which making paper records can become an end in itself. It was pointed out that this was not an inevitable consequence of PBO and should be avoided. Nonetheless it is essential for records to be maintained, as this is the only means by which evaluation can be done.

During the implementation of action plans it is equally important to maintain some key records, as it cannot be assumed that the directions or instructions given to staff can, or will, be followed. For example, when the action plan for the Truancy Project was being considered, accurate figures were not available for the number of truants who may have been on the streets during daytime hours. In choosing the action plan, it was also estimated that officers would have discretionary time available during which checks could be carried out. When the plan is implemented, records must be maintained to show when and where observations are made on juveniles, to establish that these checks are being conducted. If they are not, then it must be asked if this is because there are very few juveniles on the street, or because there is no time for officers to spend on this work.

An action plan in relation to public tranquillity proposed that officers should park their cars at conspicuous points in the vicinity of premises, such as public houses and youth clubs, which gave rise to disorderly behaviour. If no reduction is recorded in the number of complaints received from citizens, it must be established whether officers were able to carry through this action plan. If they were, then there is evidence that the strategy is not a means by which these complaints can be reduced, and the activity can be stopped. However the lack of results may have been the result of the officers not having sufficient time to spend at these locations, or they may well have visited them, but within a few minutes were sent away to answer a call. The records must reflect these circumstances and this may lead to modifications of the action plan.

Establishing Procedures

Where action plans involve officers using discretionary time to perform certain activities, the problems which were described above must be managed. Where officers are directed to patrol particular areas either in cars or on foot, or are required to make contact with individuals, or to visit community groups, then policy must establish whether these activities will have the same priority as a non-urgent call for assistance. What rules will apply to these activities when a controller requires a vehicle or a foot patrol officer to service a call? Can he redirect officers engaged on these activities or will he only redirect officers when the call is a matter of life or death? These questions cannot be answered by this book but must be addressed on the sub-division in order to ensure that everyone is working to the same set of rules.

Monitoring

It has already been emphasised that monitoring, and subsequent evaluation, are the radical differences between the PBO management process and other management techniques traditionally used by police forces. Nothing in the PBO process will change the fact that the police service is a disciplined organisation. However there are dangers that any monitoring and evaluation will be used as a means of 'catching out' officers. As far as possible the monitoring process must not be seen as punishment-centred. Monitoring is a key part of the responsibilities of managers and it is their primary responsibility to ensure the most efficient and effective use of resources.

If staff are not working effectively, it should not be automatically presumed that this is because they are either lazy, uncommitted or stupid. When problems do arise, the realistic manager should ask questions concerning the adequacy of the preparation, the briefing or the training of his staff, before assuming it is the individuals who are the source of the problem. It may be the shortcomings are within the plan, the organisation or its management. Monitoring and evaluation should be seen as a learning process for all concerned, and only as a last resort should they be associated with individual culpability and punishment.

There is little more that can be said about implementation but this should not be construed as indicating that it is an unimportant part of the process. The force can develop the most sophisticated management planning capacity which has ever existed but, if the implementation of action plans is carried out in a haphazard, unco-ordinated and half-hearted way, the quality of planning will not redeem the situation. The reason for saying relatively little about implementation is simply that, at street level, the activities undertaken by police officers will change minimally. The significant difference between yesterday and the future is the philosophy underlying the reasons why these activities are taking place at all.

Evaluation

Evaluation is the final stage of the management cycle and is an important source of information for future planning. A manager must develop the skills of evaluation for the day-to-day monitoring of action plans and the longer-term annual evaluation process. A distinction can be made between these two parts of the evaluation process: the day-to-day monitoring is the tactical evaluation, which may be the responsibility of several officers on the sub-division; the action planning co-ordinator is the person who is given responsibility for the tactical evaluation of the plan. Strategic evaluation is the responsibility of the sub-divisional superintendent and those officers above him.

Tactical Evaluation

The person co-ordinating the action plan will be the person responsible for informing the sub-divisional superintendent of the results being achieved. He must monitor the routine activities of the action plan, such as the recording of the observations of juveniles, the number of offences of burglary reported during the target hours and the number of offences detected. From this information and his overall knowledge of the police problems which led to implementation of the action plan, he is best placed to know when modification should be made to the plan and, in the longer run, whether the plan should be abandoned or continued.

Action planners have been urged to ensure that the officers who are being asked to work on those plans have sufficient time to perform all the related tasks. The same point can be made concerning officers with a responsibility for monitoring and evaluating action plans. If these officers do not have sufficient time to devote to these tasks, it is unreasonable to give them the responsibility. Furthermore this role of monitoring and evaluating should be given sufficient priority within the force to ensure it is not left as a task to be done when everything else has been completed. If the person responsible for evaluating is not able to perform these tasks correctly, for whatever reason, then the whole concept of planning, executing and assessing will fall into disrepute. In brief, tactical evaluation is concerned with asking the questions, 'Which police activities produce a desired result?' and 'Which police activities do not?'

Strategic Evaluation

The results of strategic evaluation are something which in the first instance affect the sub-division, but they should also be seen as being of value to the force as a whole. In effect, strategic evaluation should be an integral part of the process by which the force increases its fund of professional knowledge, and it provides the basis on which the community can judge the extent to which their expectations are being met.

As individuals, staff are able to learn by their own experience; however, as an organisation, the evidence would suggest that police forces do not learn very well by past experiences. There are examples where police forces have introduced some policing method which in the past had been introduced elsewhere and abandoned as unsuccessful. Strategic evaluation provides the process and the structure to measure results and record the assessments for the information of others. Sharing management experiences and knowledge becomes an integral part of the management process.

Methods of Evaluation

The specific methods to be used in the evaluation stage will have been suggested by the process of analysis and review which accompanied the designing of action plans. In fact, where it is necessary to obtain data before the plan is implemented, the design of the evaluation will have to have been considered during the action-planning stage. The method chosen will also depend upon the resources, information and skills available to the manager. The four methods which are described should not be seen as the only ones which are available for evaluating police methods. A manager must make his own decisions concerning his choice of evaluation method.

Before and After

One of the first steps in the initial stages of setting objectives was concerned with identifying the evidence that a problem existed. This process will identify indicators which can be developed as measures to establish the extent to which the problem exists. Consequently the very simplest form of evaluation can be comparisons of those measures used to define the problem with the same measures some time after an action plan has been implemented. A word of caution – as with all the measures suggested in this section, no one measure in isolation should be used as evidence of a particular result. However a combination of measures can provide confirmation of a positive, or negative, result.

To illustrate this point, the action plan example concerning the Truancy Project included one primary measure, the number of burglaries reported during the target hours. But the Results Management also included secondary measures – the number of juveniles seen, the number of juveniles found truanting from school and the number of burglaries detected. By using all four measures, a much clearer picture of what is happening as a result of the action plan will be produced. Whatever measures are used, they should be able to answer two management questions. First, what is being achieved by this action plan? Second, is it worth continuing the action plan?

Time Trends

One of the problems with using traditional police statistics, such as reported and detected crime, and road accident rates, is that they can rise and fall during the time periods chosen, whether these are monthly, half-yearly or annual. However, if a long period is chosen, shall we say five years, then it will be possible to plot the specific measure using trend analysis to produce a straight line graph which illustrates the underlying trend over the period. This trend analysis can then be projected into the future to give a predicted rate. Programs are available for micro-computers which will perform this type of analysis on data collected on the sub-division. Obviously there are a number of technical problems involved in producing these time trends and, furthermore, the accuracy of their prediction will always be subject to some variation. The accuracy of time trends can be improved if other factors are included. For example, it may be noticed over a five-year period that there has been an average increase of 10 per cent each year in the number of burglaries reported to the police. Further investigation of this figure might also reveal that the population of the sub-division has been increasing during the same period, owing to large-scale housing developments. Therefore, in this case, if the burglary rate is linked to the number of people living on the sub-division, the per capita burglary rate, when it is plotted, will give a more accurate prediction of future trends.

Another factor known to affect the crime rate is the number of young persons in the population. A substantial proportion of crime is committed by people between the ages of 14 and 25 years. Demographic trends within the community will increase or decrease the proportion of the population on a particular sub-division within those age groups. For example, a housing estate which was built to take overspill populations from urban centres may initially be populated by young married couples with very small children, but within 15 years those children are in the age range most likely to be involved in crime. A few years after that peak has been reached, those young people will either have moved away or may have grown out of their desire to commit crime. This sort of information can be very valuable in examining time trends in crime patterns, and it may well be useful to visit the local authority and refer to the census data available there.

Comparison Between Groups

Comparison between groups can also be called comparison between
areas or locations. In principle the method takes a group or area
where changes have been made to policing methods and compares
the results with a similar group or area where no changes have been
made. As an example, the number of uniformed foot patrol officers
could be increased on a beat as a strategy to reduce vandalism. As
this is a particularly prevalent offence and also one which occurs on
impulse, it may be very difficult to assess the impact of additional
police patrols in the short run. But if an area with similar social
characteristics on the sub-division is chosen, and here no changes in
police patrol strategy are introduced, the indicators which have been
identified as outcome measures can be compared between the two
areas.

Comparisons should only be made between two groups that are
truly comparable. For example, there would be no point in identifying a housing estate with a high level of vandalism and social disorder
and making a comparison with another housing estate which has
good amenities and a relatively low rate of vandalism and social
disorder. If thefts from vehicles was the matter under consideration
then, similarly, there would be no point in comparing an area where
substantial numbers of motor vehicles were left unattended in the
open with another area where vehicles were usually parked overnight
in garages.

Controlled Experiments

There are some similarities between a controlled experiment and
group comparison. The major difference between the two relates to
the level of sophistication of the measures. When making comparisons between groups, the approach requires two similar areas to be
identified on the sub-division, with, in one area, the policing strategy
being changed whilst, in the other area, it is held constant. Subsequently the measures taken from both groups are compared to
establish if any differences can be found.

In using controlled experiments, two separate areas are again identified, but here some relatively sophisticated measures are obtained
before any changes occur in policing. These measures are applied to
both areas and similar measures are taken at the end of a specified
period. Thus the method entails both 'before' and 'after' measuring
and comparison between groups. At its most sophisticated this strat-

egy involves the type of public attitude survey described in Chapter 6 where 1300 members of the public were questioned to determine if there was a need to change the police patrolling and deployment methods. This survey could have been repeated if any changes had been made, to evaluate the results.

This method is most useful when an action plan is concerned with changing the attitudes of members of the public towards services provided by the police. In the social survey described, the public were asked questions concerning their fear of crime and their satisfaction with the service they were receiving from the police. Although the survey is relatively sophisticated and time-consuming to complete, some less elaborate forms of social survey could be used by sub-divisions to look at specific groups within the sub-division or customers of specific core services.

Crime prevention campaigns have been relatively frequent features of police/public relations. Although these campaigns appear to be superficially related to changing the public's attitude towards the security of their property, in the long term crime prevention campaigns can only hope to be successful if they are able to convince people actually to change their behaviour. There is little point in educating people to the effect that their cars are likely to be stolen or have property stolen from them, if simultaneously we cannot encourage people to lock their cars. Being worried about the possibility of having your car stolen, in the absence of taking some positive steps to prevent it, will not discourage thieves.

Using the controlled experimentation method, it would be possible to check the proportion of insecure vehicles left in a particular car park. A crime prevention campaign could then be implemented and, during the campaign, a check could once again be made of the proportion of insecure motor vehicles. If there was found to be an increase in the proportion secured, then this would be a positive result. As crime prevention campaigns may have a limited period of influence on members of the public, it would also be useful to return some time after the campaign ceased to see if there had been a permanent change in the proportion of vehicles secured.

To summarise, there is no one 'best method' to assess the results achieved by an action plan, as the evaluation method will always be determined by the type of problem being tackled and the measures which identify the problem to the police manager in the first instance. The use of measures and the measurement strategy are matters which will exercise the imagination and innovation of members of the sub-division.

When to Evaluate

This is another question to which there is no right or wrong answer. As a generalisation, tactical evaluation may need to be done every week, but the long-term strategic evaluation may be carried out at intervals of six months or more. There is a compromise to be achieved. First, if the evaluation is conducted too soon then there may have been no time for something to occur, and it will be impossible to discover whether the action plan will produce the results desired, or whether the timescale on which the results will be produced is longer than anticipated. Second, if an action plan is not producing the desired results and is costly in manpower, then the longer it continues without modification or being abandoned the greater will be the waste of valuable resources. In establishing the timescales for evaluation, the manager must exercise professional judgement. However it should be remembered that the responsibility of the action plan co-ordinator is a continuous one, and not to be thought of as being restricted to monitoring action plans at the specified time periods. The co-ordinator should oversee these plans and monitor them on a day-to-day basis and make formal evaluations at the specified periods.

Results of the Evaluation

Obviously the central question in the evaluation process is simply, 'As a result of this action plan being implemented are we closer to achieving the objective now than we were before we started?' By answering this question, we will also implicitly answer a supplementary question: 'Was the original analysis of the problem correct?' It is important to consider this supplementary question as the action plan may have been sound in itself but applied to the wrong problem. For example, the Truancy Project was designed on the basis of an analysis which had indicated the involvement in burglaries of young people absent from school. In executing the action plan, no change may have been seen in the number of burglaries being recorded, but on the secondary measures it may be found that there were virtually no young people truanting from school. Therefore questions should not be raised primarily concerning the action plan, but regarding the information and the basis upon which the initial assessment and subsequent action plan were founded.

To answer the two questions, it is necessary to go through a series of other questions in a sequence to establish exactly what has happened to the action plan and what results have been achieved. There may be other questions which could be posed during this sequence, and they should not be excluded if they appear to be relevant and appropriate to the particular circumstances. The following checklist can be used as a general guide to the sequence:

1 Were all the tasks completed in the preparation phase?
2 Has the plan been executed?
3 How many man-hours have been used to date?
4 Are the man-hours that have been expended in accordance with those predicted in the plan?
5 Are the man-hours expended appropriate or should more or less manpower be assigned?
6 What results have been achieved against the primary measure?
7 What results have been achieved in terms of the secondary measures?
8 Do these results confirm the original analysis of the problem?
9 Have there been any adverse effects on other police actions?
10 Do the results, to date, suggest the need for any changes to the original action plan?
11 If changes are to be made, what are they and can they be achieved by sub-divisional resources?
12 Should the action plan be continued or abandoned?

Probably the most difficult question to answer is the last one, which requires a decision to be made concerning the action plan. This would not usually be a decision that should rest with the co-ordinator, but if he answers the sequence of questions which have preceded the final question, he should be able to prepare a case which will support his recommendation to continue or abandon the action plan. This final question does raise issues concerning the procedures to be adopted on the sub-division, and at what points and through what processes this decision should be made and by whom. It will be a matter for sub-divisional superintendents to decide how to review action plans, but it does seem an appropriate role for the Sub-divisional Planning Group. If the Group was excluded from this decision-making process, then the cycle of planning, implementation and evaluation would be effectively broken.

Strategic Evaluation

The process which produced the action plans can be seen as fanning out from the mission, through a small number of goals to a larger number of objectives, to many action plans. The process of evaluation is the reverse of this process. The results from many action plans are aggregated to each objective; these results are then focused into the goals, finally leading to the assessment of the extent to which the mission of meeting community expectations has been achieved.

The first tier of the strategic evaluation will be completed on the sub-division by the Sub-divisional Planning Group reviewing the results from all action plans and assessing their achievements against the objectives. The point during the year when this work is done will depend on local circumstances. It may be necessary to undertake some evaluation prior to the preparation of the budget bid to the police authority. If the planning year is the same as the financial year, it may be necessary to complete an interim review during December to provide the Chief Constable with information for his annual report. There may also be benefits from preparing quarterly reports for sub-divisional consultative committees. Irrespective of the timing, the process is similar.

The sub-divisional superintendent will prepare an evaluation report based on the results from individual action plans, which will show the achievements that have been made under each objective. Remember this is not a process which is judged by 'scoring points'. It is a professional management exercise in which it is of equal value to have made *no* progress towards achieving an objective, providing it is possible to give reasons, as it is to have recorded a decrease in reported crime. Of course the latter is the preferred result, but it is more important for a manager to know 'why' or 'how' something occurred than merely to know that it happened.

The report will be prepared by taking each objective in turn and then looking at all the action plans which have been set to pursue that objective. The results achieved can be added together to give an overall assessment of the sub-division's achievements. Other data may also be available to add to the assessment. Consider the objective which was set in Chapter 9 to reduce burglaries in dwelling houses by 10 per cent. Action plans would have been proposed and implemented with varying degrees of success, measured by the reduction that occurred in the numbers of reported burglaries. The number of these crimes which occurred in the daytime may have been substantially reduced by the Truancy Project, but there may have been an increase in evening burglaries. All these facts must be gathered to provide the overall assessment against the objective and also to provide the evidence to plan policing strategy for the next year. The evidence which is produced in the evaluation process may show that the nature of the problem relating to burglaries has changed following successful police operations. These new facts must form the basis of the plans for next year. Each objective will be reviewed in turn and assessed under four headings:

1 The extent to which the objective was achieved.
2 The contributions which were made by individual action plans to the achievement of the objective.
3 The current nature of the policing problem, identifying any changes which have occurred in the past year which may require specific police responses. The answer to this point will draw on the process of consultation, which will identify the needs and priorities of the community.
4 The quality of the management of action plans identifying any changes which should be considered during the next management cycle.

By making a commitment to meeting community expectations the police have, by implication, given a central role to evaluation. In the past there has been an assumption that police activities *do* achieve the desired results, so evaluation has been considered superfluous. In the disciplined and structured approach to service delivery which is summarised in the management cycle (Figure 2.1) evaluation is critical, both to the future development of the force and to demonstrate a commitment to providing excellent services to the community. Therefore the evaluation reports prepared by sub-divisions have a number of functions:

1 *Sub-divisional debriefing* The debriefing process is the opportunity to learn about successes and failures. If the sub-division is to be more effective in the future and not repeat yesterday's errors, the evaluation report should be studied and these factors identified. It is simply not good enough for an evaluation to describe what happened; the critical question is *why*? The debriefing process can tap one of the least explored sources of operational information.
2 *Sub-divisional planning* Following the debriefing, the evaluation process should feed directly to the next management cycle by

providing the starting-point for planning the next phase of community problem solving. Where an action plan has been successful in resolving a problem on one area of the sub-division, it can be adopted on another area experiencing a similar problem. The evaluation process can provide a source of effective plans which can reduce the time spent on detailed planning in future years.

3 *Marketing results to the community*   To be successful, community consultation must be a two-way process. In the first instance, the process provides a forum to identify those issues which the community believes the police have some responsibility to solve. However it is equally important to use this forum to market the results of police actions. Public confidence in the police will be more influenced by results than by pious promises for the future.

4 *Briefing   headquarters   departments* Although   headquarters departments do not have many direct responsibilities for service delivery on sub-divisions, they are responsible for developing strategic policy in areas such as crime investigation, crime prevention and road safety. The sub-divisional evaluation reports provide valuable information to assist these departments in understanding current problems and in reviewing the effectiveness of a wide range of tactics. This information provides useful insights as to their policy development roles. The report may also identify opportunities for departments to improve their service to sub-divisions.

Corporate Evaluation

Action plans on sub-divisions are linked directly to the goals in the corporate plan. The process of aggregating the results of several action plans to one objective has to be repeated, with the results of several sub-divisional objectives being linked to the relevant goal. This task is the responsibility of the department which prepared the corporate plan. All the sub-divisional evaluation reports will be reviewed to produce a corporate assessment of the extent to which the force responded to and solved community problems. Any comments about the reports made by departments would be considered in this assessment.

The evaluation reports will include comments on:

1 The extent to which the goal was achieved.
2 The contributions that were made by the various policing methods which had been adopted.

3 The current nature of the policing problem, making specific reference to any changes which have occurred which require changes in the police response or the priorities governing the allocation of resources.
4 Any management or organisational development issues which have been identified in the process.
5 Any policy issues which must be considered in the next management cycle when the corporate plan is being prepared.

The value of this process will be seen in the ability of the force to answer questions which may be raised by Her Majesty's Inspectors of Constabulary, the Police Authority or local consultative committees. Some aspects of community problem solving will respond to traditional policing tactics, but the more intractable problems will require imaginative and innovative solutions over considerable periods. If there is no commitment to develop a disciplined and structured approach to community problems, underlying social issues will not be resolved and furthermore the police will continue to be seen as the only agency responsible and to be failing to provide solutions. The corporate plan must be seen as a dynamic document which each year raises more challenges to be overcome. Such a document cannot be produced if, each year it is written, there is no reference to the achievements of the past. Therefore evaluation of past performance must become the first stage in planning for the future.

12 Meeting Community Expectations: Maintaining the Commitment

In Chapter 11, the importance of evaluating the results of sub-divisional action plans was stressed. The process of evaluation included the review of sub-divisional reports by the department responsible for preparing the corporate plan. In this chapter the broader aspects of evaluation will be described in the context of the continuing development of the force. The initial corporate plan was examined in the context of the information which had been produced by the analysis of the information which had been collected in the audit processes described in Chapters 5, 6 and 7. The modified corporate plan and the goals formed the basis of internal developments, the definition of delivery standards for certain core services and the response to community problems. The corporate evaluation will assess progress towards all the goals, based on the experience of one year. The progress or lack of progress identified by the corporate evaluation is the starting-point for planning developments for the future. The importance of building on experience of the past cannot be overstated. Therefore the responsibility for bringing together the information and producing the corporate plan should be assigned to a person of chief officer rank who will work through a department with the specific remit for this work.

The key points of this chapter are:

1 To understand the need to collate a wide range of information within the context of the corporate evaluation to provide the foundation for future developments.
2 To understand the need to assess the contribution that the management system has made to the achievements of the force.
3 To understand that a management system cannot guarantee results, it can only facilitate the achievements.
4 To understand the essential elements and issues on which the development process is based.

5 To understand the impact of the resistance to change.
6 To understand the critical success factors in organisational development.

Corporate Evaluation

The evaluation process will return to the four key questions: (1) where are we now? (2) where do we want to be in the future? (3) what progress has been made towards the vision?; and (4) what else needs to be done? Without answering these questions, the force cannot claim to have a corporate planning process because any plan produced without this discipline will not have a foundation on which to rest. The plan will simply be a shot in the dark.

Where Are We Now?

The audits of the culture and management style, the delivery standards of core services and the community expectations provided the base-line information on which this question could be answered. In Chapter 8, this information was used to plan the way forward towards the mission of meeting community expectations. Realistically the process will take time and, therefore, an incremental approach was advocated, with goals being set to identify the achievement of measurable steps. The question will therefore be answered within the context of the analysis of the initial audits. In addition to using the information provided by sub-divisions and departments, the team responsible for the corporate plan may have to repeat surveys which were conducted in the original audits. For example, the role of the culture and management style may require a further survey of staff to determine whether positive changes have occurred in their perceptions. In addition, further surveys of customer groups may be the responsibility of the corporate planning team. The corporate evaluation must have data which will establish the extent to which all the goals which were set have been achieved.

Where Do We Want to Be in the Future?

The vision which formed the basis of the answer to this question is unlikely to have changed during this initial development period, which would be no more than a year. However, as a matter of policy, the vision should be reviewed at regular intervals as part of the corporate planning process. There may be circumstances which have caused priorities to be modified; new responsibilities may have been imposed by legislation and so forth. If they do not make the conscious effort to look at the world in the widest context, police services will eventually be out of step with the community. Even where no changes are required, the act of examining and restating the vision brings it to the fore at the start of the corporate planning process.

What Progress Has Been Made Towards the Vision?

By answering question (2) the target has been confirmed, thus enabling this question to be answered. Even if there has been some modification to the vision, this question can be answered because it is the first step in the planning stage of the new management cycle. The start has been made to convert the information from the evaluation of last year's achievements to the base-line for next year's planning and actions. By recognising the cyclical nature of the process, the evaluation report becomes a valuable resource, not simply something to help the Chief Constable with his annual report.

What Else Needs to Be Done?

The answers to the first three questions provide an assessment of the current position of the force in relation to the vision. Even if there have been some changes to which the force has to respond, these have been considered by answering the second question. Finally the experience gained through the corporate evaluation provides the foundation on which to develop targets for the coming year. The initial response to this question can be seen as the process of setting provisional goals, using the framework described in Chapter 4. This initial assessment should then be followed by a process of consultation and working groups, if necessary, to develop options to make further progress towards the vision. The basis of this process was described in Chapter 8; in the second and subsequent years the procedures may become less elaborate, but the rigour and discipline of the system must be maintained. Decisions concerning priorities and resources must be subjected to the same objective analysis to ensure that the meeting of community expectations is the overriding concern.

Learning from Experience

The audits of community expectations and service delivery standards and the evaluation of the extent to which community problems have been solved will have provided the base-line on which to measure success, but the critical factor affecting the achievement of success will be the extent to which the mission of the force has been embraced by the staff. A principal purpose of the audit of the culture and management style was to determine the factors inhibiting staff from achieving their full potential. The literature on management development consistently provides evidence of the extent to which changes have to occur in the culture and management style to enable the mission to be achieved.

Chapter 5 included a checklist of issues which managers were encouraged to use to identify the culture and style of their own sphere of command. The relative importance of each element should have been determined and, where it was seen to have an adverse effect on the achievements of the sub-division or department, remedial action was recommended. During the evaluation phase the same review should be carried out to determine whether the original problems had been resolved and to see if new ones had arisen. When conducting this review a distinction should be made between problems which can be traced back to the preparation phase before changes were made to the organisation and those which appear to have occurred during implementation.

The system of management will only be as good as the people who direct and participate in the process. The force needs people to make progress towards the vision, but those same people can also prevent those improvements being achieved. The structured and disciplined approach to management development which has been described in this book can only *facilitate* improvements on performance – it cannot guarantee results. The corporate evaluation must ask questions about the degree of understanding which exists within the force concerning the changes which have occurred. The commitment of all staff to the mission must be assessed. The degree of trust between staff and their perceptions of their work will also form part of this evaluation.

Question 1   Do the Members of the Force have Sufficient Understanding of the Development Process?

Members of the force should have realised why changes were being made to adopt service delivery standards and the commitment to meeting community expectations, as well as the consequences of these changes. If some staff or groups of staff believed they could stand aside and not become involved, the total nature of the commitment which was required has not been understood. It would be very difficult for staff to make the maximum contribution to the force if they did not know or understand why changes had been made. Staff must undertake their roles within the system and have a clear definition of their responsibilities and authority. If there were problems in relation to the understanding of what was expected of them, the preparation strategy should be examined to determine if there was a need for additional training. The most likely cause of this problem is the quality of the communication systems and methods. If, a year after implementation, there are still staff who do not understand the mission and the reasons behind the changes, the feedback mechanisms from staff to managers either do not exist or are suspect, because a sensitive manager should have recognised the problem sooner. Whatever the cause, a lack of understanding of the mission will make a real commitment by staff to meeting community expectations virtually impossible.

Question 2   Does the Mission Enjoy the Support and Commitment of the Chief Constable and his Executive Management?

Some might claim that the support and commitment of the Chief Constable is the single most important factor for the process of organisational change. On its own it will not guarantee success, but if it is absent then there is very little chance of success. Let us be clear what achieving the mission demands: it is making the force and individual staff responsible for meeting community expectations by determining priorities, establishing targets to be achieved and then evaluating results. In short, it is adopting a system which can identify failures of achievement and identify the groups of staff who are responsible. The fear of failure is a very powerful motivation to do nothing. Why should officers expose themselves to the chance of failure if they have doubts about the commitment of their leaders? If they do not achieve the success they hoped, then they should be able to rely on their managers to understand the reasons for failure.

Support will be demonstrated in a variety of ways. The training which must accompany the preparation for change will raise issues of policy, resources and the delegated authority to make decisions. Many of these questions can only be answered by officers who are involved in the executive management of the force. If these officers do not contribute on a continuing basis to these training courses by being present, then these matters will remain unresolved and the entire training and preparation process may be significantly damaged. The pre-implementation training provides opportunities for staff to learn about the proposed changes and for executive management to become better informed of staff's anxieties, their lack of understanding and any gaps that may exist in planning and policy which must be addressed before implementation. One of the most tangible examples of top-level support is when staff obtain the resources which have been identified as a necessary prerequisite for success. If a force cannot provide the agreed resources, it has built in the excuse for failure. Overt support must continue throughout the implementation phase, with care being taken not to allow enthusiasm and support to become interference with the operational autonomy which has been established by policy.

Question 3   Did the Mission Receive Commitment and Active Support Throughout the Force?

The commitment and support of the Chief Constable is essential to the success of the venture and should act as an example of good management practice to the rest of the force. However the Chief Constable must expect and receive the active support and commitment of all staff. Problems will occur if some parts of the force believe they are exempt from a drive to meet community expectations. Selection for promotion should reflect the new management needs of the force and seek the means of identifying those staff with real commitment who do not merely pay lip-service to the achievement of excellent standards. If staff in senior management positions lack commitment, the system of accountability and responsibility should be examined and modified accordingly. If they can continue to remain outside the corporate efforts of the rest of the force, the evaluation systems may need tightening to encourage these officers to co-operate or to be seen to be abdicating their responsibilities.

Question 4   Does Trust Exist Between Members of the Force?

An important means of reducing the fear of failure in any new venture is to generate a climate of mutual trust. The Chief Constable may tell the force that he does not expect instant success on every goal, but that he is realistic enough to recognise that success in some areas will not be equalled in others. Despite this public statement, if his staff do not trust him they will still fear the consequences of failure and may even subvert the process by 'fixing' the figures or not setting any challenging objectives.

Trust is also a critical issue in the decision-making process. The management process which has been described argues for decision making to occur as close to the problem and sources of information as possible. In most police forces this would require some devolution of decision making from a central point in the organisation to lower levels within the force. In fact the proposals made in this book would make the sub-division the basic operational unit and the policy would give more scope for decision making at that level. Inevitably errors in decision making will occur, but this can happen anywhere in the organisation and the urge to return to centralised decision making must be resisted. Trust and adequate training should be the foundations of the decision-making system.

Question 5 *Have There Been any Changes in the Officers' Perceptions of Their Work?*

It will be misleading to overemphasise the apparent differences and conflicts which exist between staff and their supervisors. However the organisational culture and style, staff morale and job satisfaction can be damaged by this conflict. Where a manager is asking his staff to change their working practices or to take on additional work, he should try and identify the advantages that this will bring to them. If no advantages can be demonstrated, it should come as no surprise if the staff resist the changes. Managers have a responsibility to promote the positive aspects of the need to change working arrangements; therefore changes in the staff's perceptions of their work will give a good indication of the success or failure of the organisational changes. The following aspects of the work should have become more positive:

1　Staff should have a greater sense of involvement in the policy making of the force and the design of service delivery methods.
2　Staff should be able to understand how their work contributes to the overall strategies and achievements of the force.
3　Staff should feel more confident about their own abilities and should gain a sense of achievement from their work.
4　Staff should have a greater sense of personal responsibility towards the use of resources, including their own time.

In Chapter 5, the predominantly hierarchical and authoritarian structures of police forces were seen to be at variance with the needs of the staff who deliver services. The process of meeting community expectations, if successfully implemented, will modify the management philosophy of the force to make it more suitable for the needs of its staff. Police work demands particular attitudes and behaviours from staff. Managers should seek to modify management philosophy to coincide with the needs of staff.

Resistance to Change

Throughout the force there may be a positive response by most staff to the changes required by the new management strategy, but some individuals may adopt attitudes or responses which have the potential to inhibit or prevent the achievement of all the possible improvements to the force. Resistance to change is a natural human response. The development process which has been advocated will reduce the degree of resistance because the changes which occur in the force will have been the product of the efforts of all staff.

The fact-finding exercise and the planning process demand consultation between staff and an involvement of many. The corporate plan is an unambiguous symbol of the Chief Constable's commitment to the process of meeting community expectations. It also forms a contract between him and the force by identifying the support he will give to the efforts of his staff. Therefore the force is guided and motivated by overt leadership and a shared sense of mission.

The style of management which has been described follows a learning approach. Managers must ensure that this style is not lost in the evaluation process, to be replaced by a punitive and critical assessment of police performance. Where achievements have fallen short of the targets which were set, managers should look for reasons rather than seeking to blame individuals. The rational management approach is concerned with achieving operational improvements, which are likely to facilitate improved human relations. Therefore improved policing methods should be accompanied by improvements in the interpersonal skills of all officers with managerial responsibilities.

Some resistance to change is inevitable and managers have the responsibility to be prepared to resolve problems as they occur. Therefore, before a manager can address problems associated with resistance to change, he must have sufficient time and possess the necessary interpersonal skills. Any single issue might take many hours of counselling, policy review and on-the-job training to resolve. Managers must have the skills to listen to their staff. They must have an empathy with staff who are anxious about their new roles which should be balanced by the need to make progress towards the changes required to achieve the meeting of community expectations. If the force is not prepared to make time available to managers at every level for these tasks or to provide the training for the development of skills, then the chances of the force achieving its mission will be reduced. Management development is a package which only delivers results if all the parts are included.

Meeting Community Expectations in a Changing World

The theme throughout this book has been the commitment to meeting community expectations. More sophisticated customers, increased demand both in terms of quantity and quality, and limited resources require Chief Constables to make decisions about priorities. Unless there is some objective context in which to make these decisions, they are open to criticisms of being arbitrary and biased. If however, the Chief Constable can point to a link between his decisions and the expectations of the community, then he is less open to challenge. Given the propensity for society to change it seems sensible to have a ... sion on which to base consistent and objective decision making. In the past the emphasis has been on conducting 'business as usual', with changes to policing methods occurring as almost spontaneous responses to individual problems. This approach will not be adequate in the future because the success of this method as a means of improving police performance is extremely suspect. Police forces will continue to conduct business as usual, but in addition they will have a vision of the future which will form the basis of the strategy to achieve goals on the route to the vision. Furthermore they will cease to make assumptions that police activities have a value in themselves; the emphasis will be on the evaluation of the results produced in the context of meeting community expectations.

In the initial stages of achieving improvements in performance, the force will experience quite radical changes. These changes will be seen in the structures of the force, the roles and responsibilities of individual officers and civilians, the roles and relationships between parts of the force, and the introduction of new systems and technology. After the initial surge which accompanies these changes, the force will settle back to sustain the improvements which have been achieved and make further progress through the pursuit of a structured and disciplined process exemplified by the management cycle. In fact the process of management which has been described will provide the mechanism for sustained improvements in performance to achieve the vision and the framework for the force to respond to the changing world. There is a danger that the force will believe that it is now committed to a permanent state of uncertainty and change. It will be true that the management philosophy of the force must accept the need to examine new problems as they arise and seek novel solutions, but this should be seen as a natural extension of the management process and not as a matter which should be associated with uncertainty and anxiety. To reduce the anxieties which are associated with change, the force should build on the experience of each year and check progress against the long-term vision. This will give a sense of continuity and coherence to the developments. Additionally staff should be involved at all times to ensure continued understanding and opportunities to influence policy.

The fact-finding exercise which formed the foundation on which the developments have been based provided a unique learning experience for all staff. However the achievements of sub-divisions and departments will be influenced by the knowledge and skills of individuals. Therefore an important part of the corporate evaluation is to identify the limitation on achievements which has been caused by factors related to individual skills and competence. This should then form part of a counselling, training and personal development programme for the individuals concerned.

The Characteristics of Successful Management Innovations

Improvements in the performance and quality of police services will not occur overnight by accident or chance. They will be achieved by professional and competent management which should be capable of learning from the experience of others. A study by the Rand Corporation examined the characteristics of successful innovations in the field of criminal justice, which included police forces, and identified six critical success factors:[1]

1   All members of the force should share a sincere motivation to achieve the mission of the organisation. Where the members of

the force are responsible for analysing existing performance and are able to propose methods for improvements, then commitment and motivation to change are more likely to occur. Where people do not see the need for change their commitment will always be suspect.

2   The study used the phrase 'key actor support' to identify the need to have the active leadership and commitment of the head of the organisation and also people who are located at various critical points within the organisation. An important part of the preparation process is to identify the key personnel and to ensure their understanding and active commitment.

3   Closely related to the support of key personnel is the skill and competence of these participants in the process. Commitment alone will not bring success. Where people are being called upon to perform new and more demanding roles they must receive appropriate training. There can be a few more threatening situations than to be asked to do something but not be given the skills to respond.

4   Where participants are being asked to change their working practices or undertake a more demanding role they will expect to see some advantages to them for responding. In short they must be able to see some benefits if they are to be expected to accept the costs of the change. The study found that monetary rewards were not necessarily strong motivators. People were more likely to respond to the more intangible benefits of having more challenging work, the satisfaction which could be gained by knowing they had achieved an objective and the feelings of being personally involved in the problem-solving process.

5   Improvements in organisational effectiveness were more likely to occur where the participants had a clear definition of the goals they were seeking to achieve. It was not enough simply to state goals; they had to be defined unambiguously in terms which enabled staff to understand what was expected of them and how they would know when the goals had been achieved.

6   Finally clear lines of authority were found to have a significant influence on the improvements which could be achieved through organisational change.

All the key ingredients found by the Rand Corporation study have been addressed. The method which the force adopts to initiate the process of change will be critical in generating the support, motivation and commitment of the staff. If the Chief Constable and his executive management do not lead from the front and demonstrate their commitment to the process, then it is likely to be still-born and to fail to achieve any tangible improvements in performance both in terms of effectiveness and quality of the services provided.

It is worth recalling the comments made about Unit Beat Policing in Chapter 2. There is nothing to stop a Chief Constable responding to criticism of his force by issuing a statement that he is adopting 'total quality management' or some new system of police deployment, or by publishing a mission statement. However, without showing evidence to link it to the needs of his community and to having a system which will ensure results are achieved, he will do little in the long term for the good of the community or the image of the police service. If there is one message it is to recognise that 'saying and doing' is not enough – it is results that count, and results which are linked to the community's needs and expectations.

Before embarking on the implementation of changes to meet community expectations, it may be worth considering the conversation Alice in Wonderland had with the Cheshire Cat.

> Alice said to the cat, 'Would you tell me please which way I ought to go from here?'
> 'That depends a good deal on where you want to go,' said the cat.
> 'I don't much care where,' said Alice.
> 'Then it doesn't much matter which way you go,' said the cat.

A Chief Constable may realise he has to make progress, but without knowing where he is starting from and without a vision of where he wants to go, he will undertake a mystery tour. However, unlike Alice, who travelled alone, the Chief Constable will be accompanied by several million pounds' worth of expensive resources.

Note

1   P. Ellickson, J. Petersilia, M. Saggiano and S. Polin, *Implementing New Ideas in Criminal Justice*, Santa Monica, California: Rand Corporation (1983).

Index